easy

Access 97
Second Edition

See it done

Do it yourself

que®

W9-BIP-256

Part ▷ 1: Learning the Basics

Part ▷ 2: Designing and Creating an Access Database

Copyright© 1999 by Que® Corporation

International Standard Book Number: 0-7897-1822-7

Library of Congress Catalog Card Number: 98-86623

Printed in the United States of America

First Printing: November, 1998

00 99 98   4   3   2   1

Trademarks

All terms mentioned in this book that are known to be trademarks or service marks have been appropriately capitalized. Que Corporation cannot attest to the accuracy of this information. Use of a term in this book should not be regarded as affecting the validity of any trademark or service mark. Access is a registered trademark of Microsoft Corporation.

Warning and Disclaimer

Every effort has been made to make this book as complete and as accurate as possible, but no warranty or fitness is implied. The information provided is on an "as is" basis. The authors and the publisher shall have neither liability nor responsibility to any person or entity with respect to any loss or damages arising from the information contained in this book.

About the Author

Jeffry Byrne has been working and teaching about computers, and particularly about database applications, for over 15 years. He is the author of numerous computer software books in several languages, including *Paradox QuickStart*, *Using CA-Simply Money, Easy Access for Windows, Easy Access for Windows 95, Easy Access 97*, and now *Easy Access 97, Second Edition*. He has also contributed to *Using QuickBooks for Windows* and *Using PowerPoint 4*. In addition, he has written several other books on Microsoft SQL Server and other popular database and spreadsheet applications. When not writing about and testing software, Jeff works as a System Administrator for a manufacturing company in Portland, Oregon. Jeff can be contacted at jeffbyrne@cnnw.net.

Dedication

First and foremost, all my thanks and love go to my wife Marisa, who put up with the late nights and considerable neglect so that I could finish this project. Without your belief in me I would not have come so far.

Acknowledgements

Thanks to all the people at Macmillan Computer Publishing who had a hand in this book. I know that there are many of you whom I have never talked with. Special thanks go to Rosemarie Graham for asking me to do the latest revision of this work, to Matt Purcell for answering my questions and his dedication to ensuring that everything got done on time, and Tonya Simpson with all the help in editing.

Executive Editor
Rosemarie Graham

Acquisitions Editor
Rosemarie Graham

Development Editor
Matt Purcell

Managing Editor
Jodi Jensen

Project Editor
Tonya Simpson

Indexer
Christine Nelsen

Technical Editor
Dallas Releford

Production Designer
Trina Wurst

Proofreader
Mona Brown

Book Designer
Jean Bisesi

Cover Designers
Anne Jones
Karen Ruggles

Illustrations
Bruce Dean

How to Use This Book

It's as Easy as 1-2-3

Each part of this book is made up of a series of short, instructional lessons, designed to help you understand basic information that you need to get the most out of your computer hardware and software.

① Each step is fully illustrated to show you how it looks onscreen.

Click: Click the left mouse button once.

Double-click: Click the left mouse button twice in rapid succession.

Right-click: Click the right mouse button once.

Pointer Arrow: Highlights an item on the screen you need to point to or focus on in the step or task.

Selection: Highlights the area onscreen discussed in the step or task.

Click & Type: Click once where indicated and begin typing to enter your text or data.

✓ Tips and ① Warnings give you a heads-up for any extra information you may need while working through the task.

② Each task includes a series of quick, easy steps designed to guide you through the procedure.

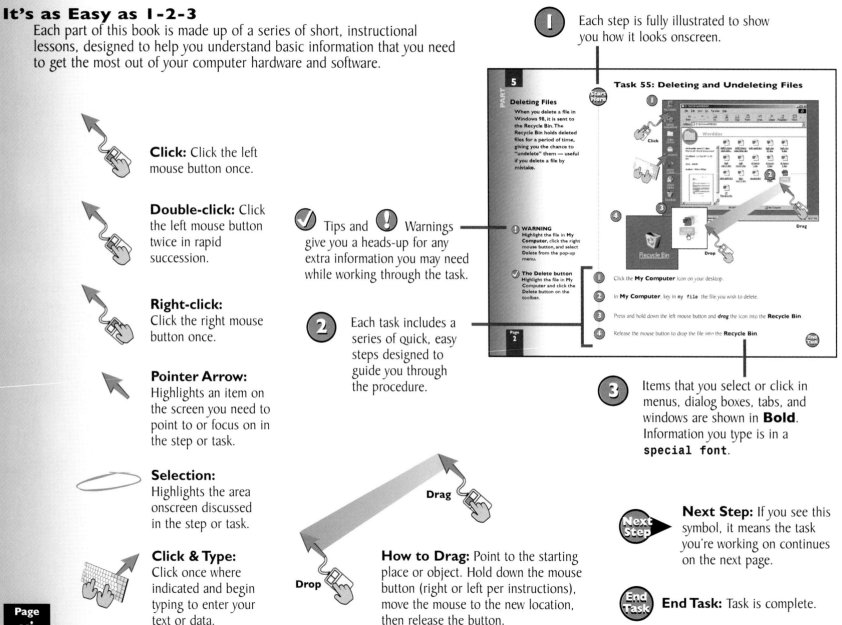

③ Items that you select or click in menus, dialog boxes, tabs, and windows are shown in Bold. Information you type is in a special font.

Drag

Drop

How to Drag: Point to the starting place or object. Hold down the mouse button (right or left per instructions), move the mouse to the new location, then release the button.

Next Step: If you see this symbol, it means the task you're working on continues on the next page.

End Task: Task is complete.

Introduction to Easy Access 97, 2nd Edition

A database program is probably the most complex piece of software that you will ever use—but it doesn't have to be. In this book you will learn to create your own database and add information into tables. Then you can build forms to view your information in a format with which you are familiar. In order to find information located in the database, you will create queries to ask questions and find the specific data you need. Finally, you will learn to print reports from the information in the database.

Although there is much for you to learn when you use Access 97, this book will lead you step by step through the process. Each task throughout this book shows you specifically how to accomplish the necessary job. You'll learn the simplest way to accomplish each task.

You can easily use this book as a simple reference, or read it from start to finish, working along with each task as you go. Whichever way you prefer, *Easy Access 97, Second Edition* shows you how it is done and how you can do it yourself.

Tell Us What You Think!

As the reader of this book, you are our most important critic and commentator. We value your opinion and want to know what we're doing right, what we could do better, what areas you'd like to see us publish in, and any other words of wisdom you're willing to pass our way.

As the Executive Editor for the Database team at Macmillan Computer Publishing, I welcome your comments. You can fax, email, or write me directly to let me know what you did or didn't like about this book—as well as what we can do to make our books stronger.

Please note that I cannot help you with technical problems related to the topic of this book, and that due to the high volume of mail I receive, I might not be able to reply to every message.

When you write, please be sure to include this book's title and author as well as your name and phone or fax number. I will carefully review your comments and share them with the author and editors who worked on the book.

Fax: 317-817-7070

Email: databases@mcp.com

Mail: Rosemarie Graham
       Executive Editor
       Database Team
       Macmillan Computer Publishing
       201 West 103rd Street
       Indianapolis, IN 46290 USA

PART I

Learning the Basics

In this section, you will learn to open an Access database file, to select menu commands, and to use the toolbar. You will also see how to use the Help systems, including the Office Assistant. If you already know how to open and exit programs and to use Windows 95 style menus, you can skip ahead to Task 6. If you are not familiar with these topics, be sure to work through them carefully. These tasks are applicable to almost any other Windows-type applications you might use.

Tasks

Task 1: Installing Microsoft Access 97

Before you can start to use Access, you must first install the program. If you are working at a company with some type of IS department, someone else will probably install the program for you. If this isn't the case, then you will simply install the program yourself.

First make sure that you have the Microsoft Access CD-ROM and the CD key number handy. This task assumes that you are using the Microsoft Office Professional on CD-ROM. The installation process is similar if you have purchased Microsoft Access 97 as a standalone product or have a disk-based version.

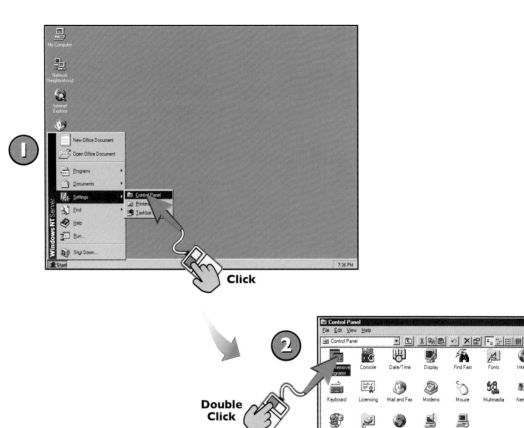

Click

Double Click

 Insert the CD-ROM with the Access program into your drive, and click the **Start** button. Click **Settings**, **Control Panel** from the menus.

Double-click the **Add/Remove Programs** applet icon.

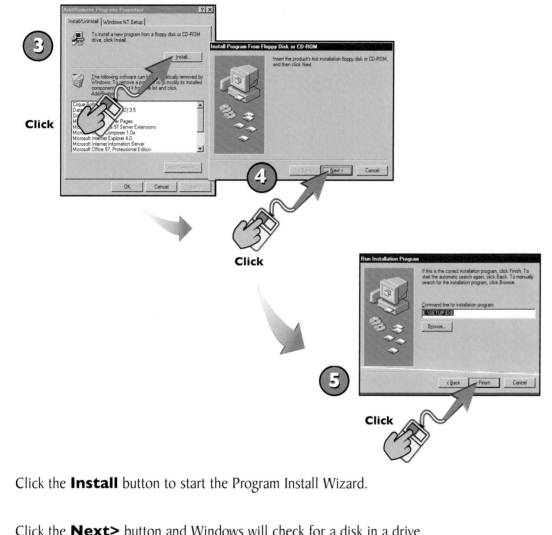

Click

Click

Click

Click

③ Click the **Install** button to start the Program Install Wizard.

④ Click the **Next>** button and Windows will check for a disk in a drive.

⑤ Click the **Finish** button.

✓ **Alternative start**
You can also start an application by clicking it once and then pressing the Enter key.

✓ **The setup program**
You should see something like **SETUP.EXE** listed in the program text box. This is the name of the setup program that will install your application.

Next Step

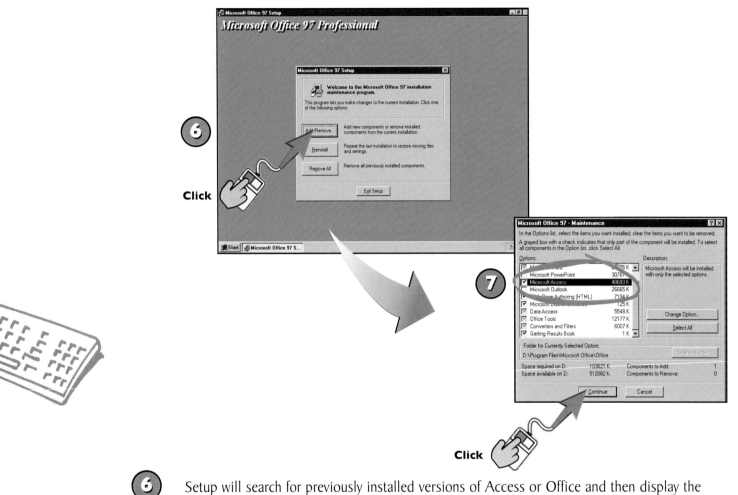

Click

Click

6 Setup will search for previously installed versions of Access or Office and then display the Welcome dialog box. Click the **Add/Remove** button to begin the installation.

7 If a check mark does not already exist in the check box beside Microsoft Access, place one there by clicking inside the box, and then click the **Continue** button.

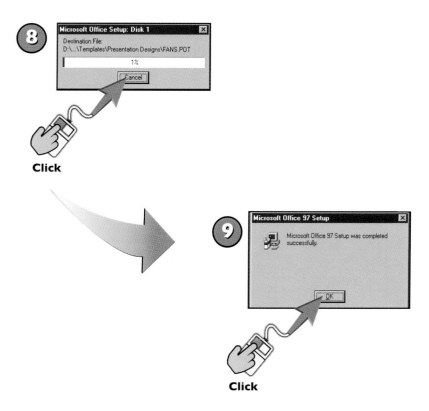

Click

Click

 A status dialog box is now displayed. If you want to cancel the installation click the **Cancel** button.

 Click the **OK** button to complete the installation.

 Normal installation
If you are installing
Microsoft Office
Professional, you can install
all the normal components
by leaving all the check
boxes at their default
settings. The default
installation includes
Access.

Task 2: Starting Access from the Start Button

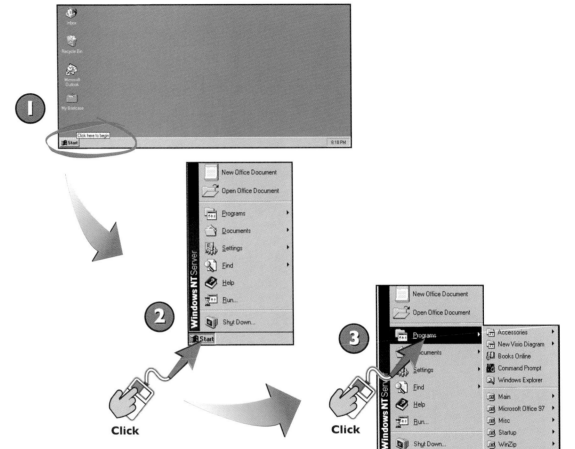

Access is a database program that works only in the Windows 95, Windows 98, or Windows NT 4 environment. After you install Access on your computer system, you can start the program from the **Start** button menus. The **Start** button is located on the taskbar at the bottom of your screen. If your taskbar is not visible, drag the mouse all the way to the bottom of your screen and see if the taskbar pops up. It might also be located at one of the other edges of your screen.

The Windows taskbar **Start** button opens a series of menus that enable you to open and work with most of the various programs and applications you have installed on your computer. Here you will use the **Start** button menus to open Access.

Click

Click

(1) When you place the mouse pointer on the **Start** button, notice the ToolTip that says **Click here to begin** floating above the button.

(2) Click the **Start** button, displaying the menu.

(3) Move the mouse up to the **Programs** option and display its submenu.

Next Step

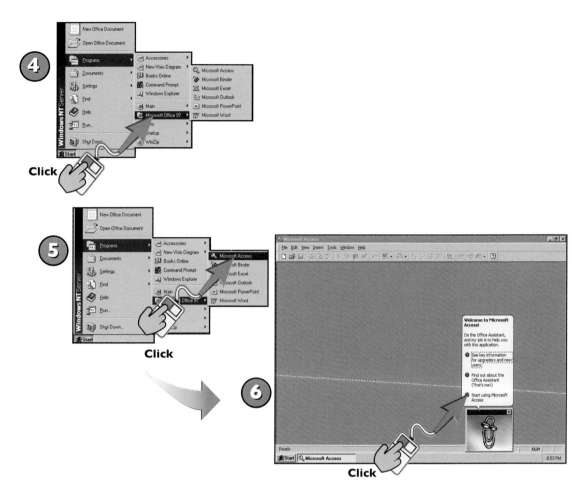

4 Move the mouse down to the **Microsoft Office 97** option and you will see a new submenu displayed.

5 Click the **Microsoft Access** option on this submenu to open the Access application.

6 Click the small blue button **Start using Microsoft Access** inside the balloon above the Office Assistant's box.

✓ **My menu is different**
Your own menu structure might be different than this example. Look for **Microsoft Access, Access 97, Office,** or **Applications** on the **Programs** and **Start** menus.

Task 3: Opening an Existing Database

In order to add data to a database file, you must first locate the file on your disk and then open it inside the Access application. When you open a database file, you gain access to the information located in the tables.

You might have more than one database file to select from, so you must know the name and location of the file that you want to use. In this task you will learn to select a database file and then open it. The sample database provided with Access, Northwind Traders, will be used for this task. It is normally installed along with the program.

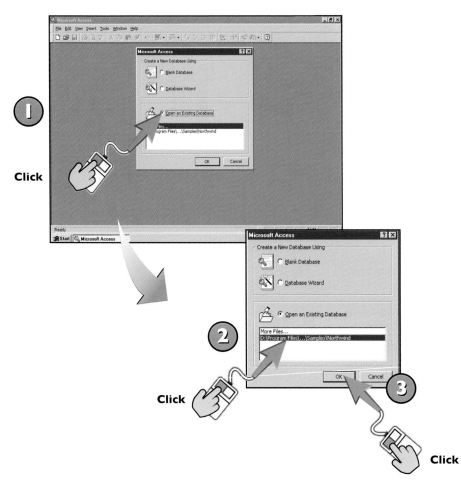

Click

Click

Click

(1) Select **Open an Existing Database** by clicking inside the option button circle. The black dot inside the circle means the option has been selected.

(2) Click the **Northwind** database name inside the list box to select the file to be opened.

(3) Click the **OK** button to open the file.

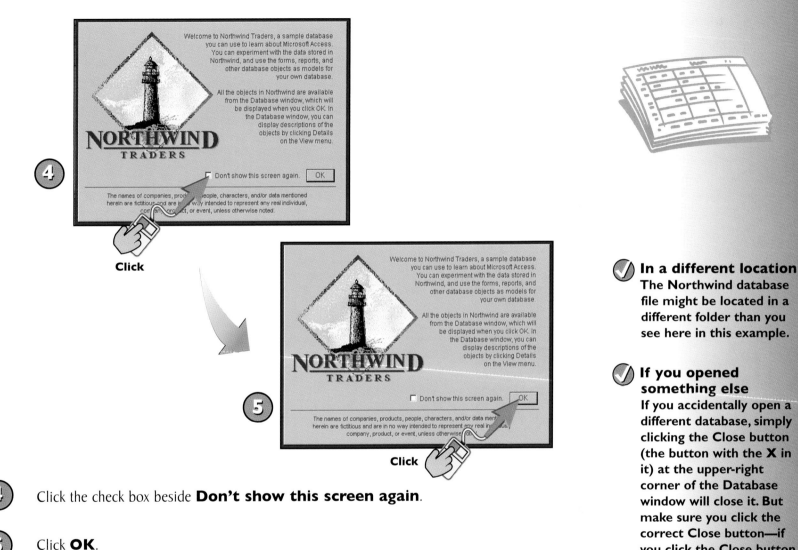

Click

Click

④ Click the check box beside **Don't show this screen again**.

⑤ Click **OK**.

✓ **In a different location**
The Northwind database file might be located in a different folder than you see here in this example.

✓ **If you opened something else**
If you accidentally open a different database, simply clicking the **Close** button (the button with the **X** in it) at the upper-right corner of the Database window will close it. But make sure you click the correct **Close** button—if you click the **Close** button on the **Access** window, the application will close and you will have to start Access again.

Task 4: Using Menu Commands

Information stored in tables can be manipulated in many ways, and this is done through various methods, many of which are accessed through menu commands.

The menu commands are accessed through the menu bar located at the top of your screen. Realize that some commands and functions are accessed through a series of menus, submenus, or dialog boxes. Unlike a menu, a dialog box often enables you to make several choices about the object you are working with, and then apply all the selections at one time. You can select menu commands and many options available in dialog boxes by using either the keyboard or the mouse. When available, a shortcut keyboard combination is displayed to the right of the command on the menu, such as Ctrl+P to print an item.

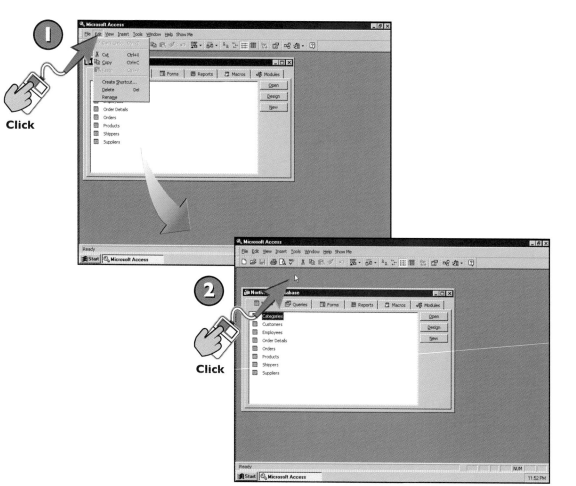

Click

Click

Click the mouse on the **Edit** option on the menu bar to display its menu.

Now move the mouse away from the menu to a blank area on the Access desktop and click once to deselect the menu.

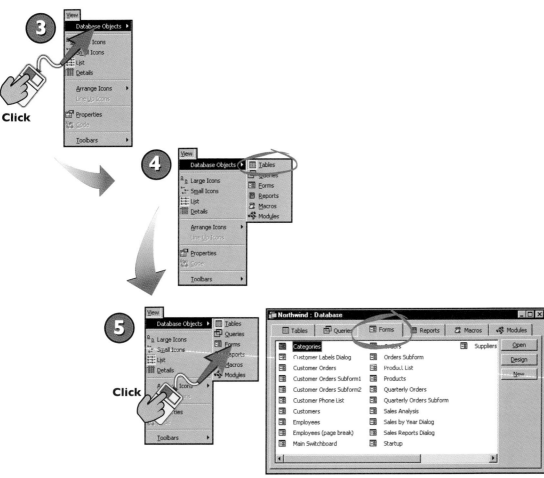

Click

Click

Keyboard shortcuts
To the right of some menu items you will see a two-key keyboard shortcut option. You can access these menu options without going through the menus by pressing the Ctrl key and then the indicated letter at the same time. Menu items that are dimmed are not available.

More shortcuts
Any time you see an underlined letter on a menu option, it is the *hotkey*. The menu item can be immediately accessed through the hotkey by holding down both the Alt key and the underlined letter on your keyboard.

3 Press the Alt key on your keyboard, activating the menu bar, and then the letter V to display the **View** menu. Click the **Database Objects** option to display its submenu.

4 You will see the list of the six Access object groups. The currently selected object is indicated by the depressed button beside its name, in this case **Tables**.

5 Click the **Forms** menu option, and see how the Database window changes from the **Tables** group to the **Forms** group.

Many commands and functions are only a single mouse click away when you use the available toolbars. Not all commands are available on a toolbar, just as not all toolbar features are represented on the menus. As you work with different objects in Access the toolbar will automatically change, adding and dropping buttons not applicable to the current object. Depending on what you are doing, Access might add secondary toolbars to your screen, giving you access to more options.

Task 5: Using Toolbar Buttons

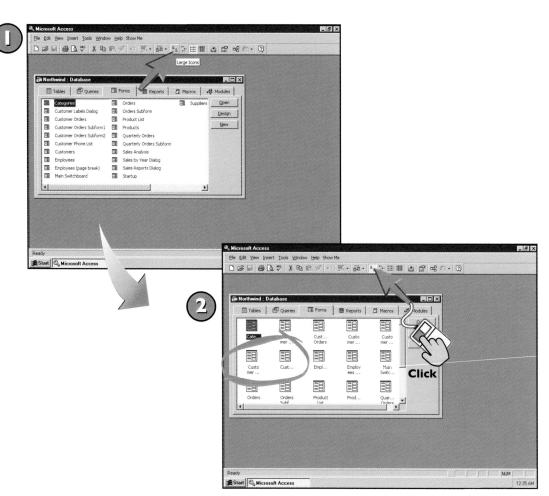

 Move the mouse pointer so that it is on the Large Icons button.

 Click the button and see how all the objects in the **Forms** window change to large icons.

✓ Using ToolTips
If you pause the mouse pointer on a toolbar button, a small ToolTip is displayed. This is to give you an idea of the use for the button.

Task 6: Using Tab Buttons

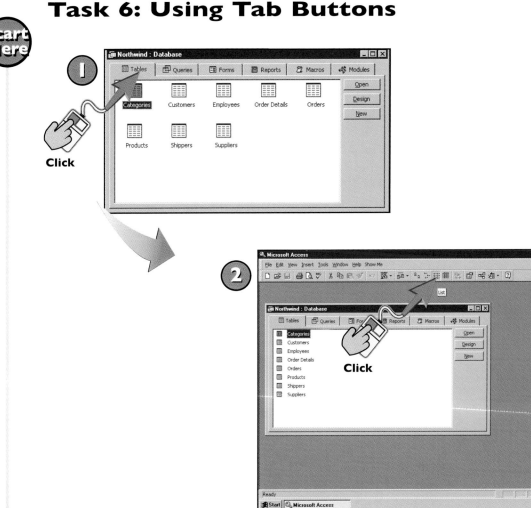

Click

Click

At the top of the Database window is a series of six tab buttons. These are used to gain access to the major object categories: tables, queries, forms, reports, macros, and modules. You must use the mouse to work with tab buttons and toolbars.

1. Click the **Tables** tab button, displaying the list of tables now shown with large icons.

2. Click the List toolbar button to change the icons back to the default List format.

✓ Using tab buttons
If you accidentally click the wrong tab button, just select another. Notice how the text color of the tab button changes to blue when the mouse pointer is on it. The tab with the blue text is the one that will be selected when you click then.

Task 7: Getting Help

Access provides several avenues to get the help you might need on its many features. In earlier days, you would receive a large manual to go with your program. Now help is limited to various help screens and methods.

Access has a very comprehensive online help that makes it very easy to find out the information you are looking for. From within the Access Help system you can choose from three major venues: a table of contents, an index, and a find system. Here you will use the table of contents help.

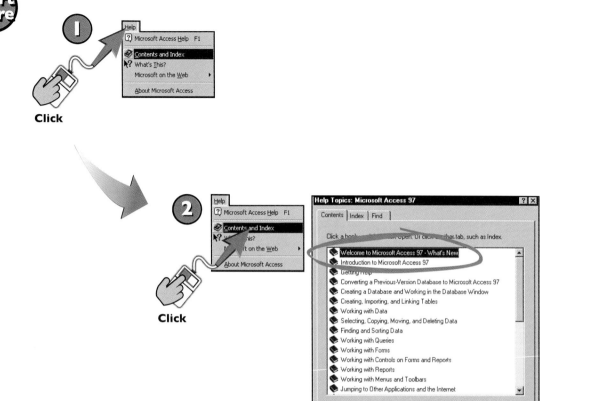

Click

Click

Click the **Help** menu option to display the Help menu.

Click the **Contents and Index** menu option to display the Help Topics dialog box.

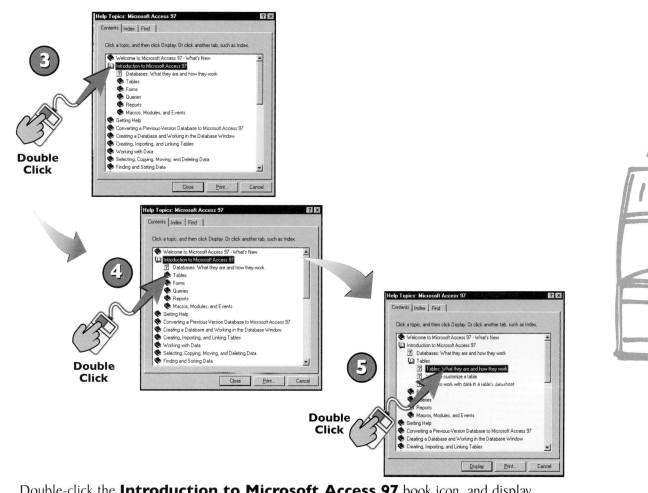

3 Double-click the **Introduction to Microsoft Access 97** book icon, and display the list of subtopics below it.

4 Double-click the subtopic icon **Tables**.

5 Double-click the topic icon **Tables: What they are and how they work** to view the information about this topic.

Getting Help Continued

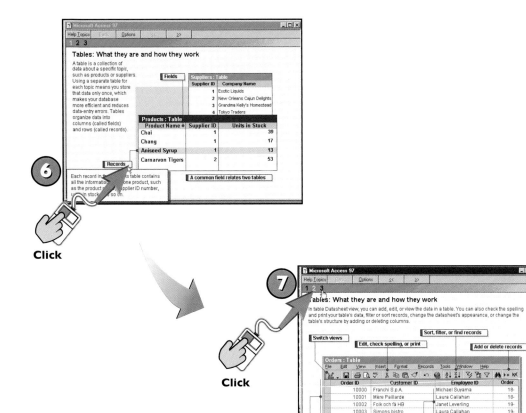

Click

Click

6 Move the mouse pointer over the **Records** callout; the pointer changes shape from an arrow to a pointing finger. Click to display a paragraph about the item being pointed out.

7 Click the number **2** beneath the menu to display the next page of the topic.

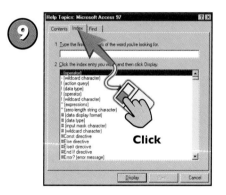

Tables: What they are and how they work

In table Datasheet view, you can add, edit, or view the data in a table. You can also check the spelling and print your table's data, filter or sort records, change the datasheet's appearance, or change the table's structure by adding or deleting columns.

Click

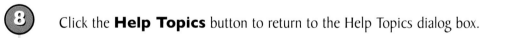

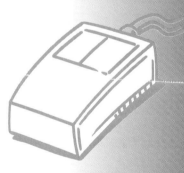

Click

---

8 Click the **Help Topics** button to return to the Help Topics dialog box.

9 Click the **Index** tab button.

Task 8: Using the Index

The Access index is an excellent method of searching for help on a specific subject. The index works much as an index in a book works—but even easier. With the index, you simply type a word or phrase and Access shows you a list of topics that relate to the item you entered.

Start Here

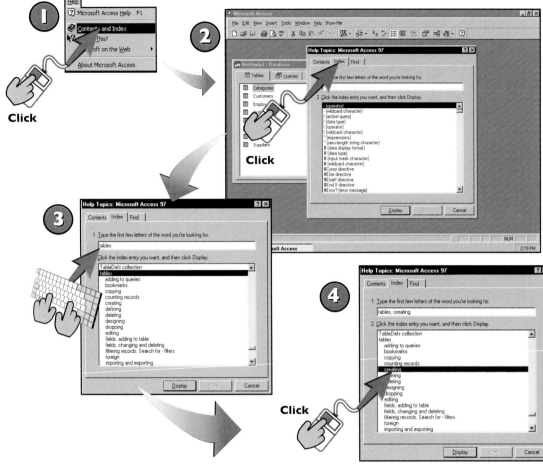

Click

Click

Click

Click

Next Step

More help with Find
The **Find** tab gives you a more extensive version of **Index**. Find enables you to type a word or phrase, and then select from several displayed options.

1 Click **Help**, **Contents and Index**.

2 Click the **Index** tab button.

3 Use the index to get help on specific topics by typing a word in the text box. Type **tables** and see the list of all help topics beginning with the word "tables" in the lower text box.

4 Click the word **creating** in the lower list to view the help topic on **tables**, **creating**. Use the horizontal scrollbar to view more topics if necessary.

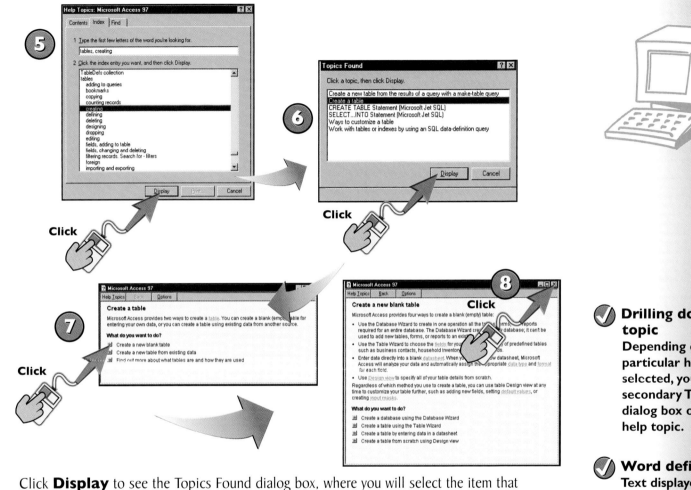

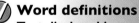

Drilling down to a topic
Depending on the particular help you have selected, you might see a secondary Topics Found dialog box or the actual help topic.

Word definitions
Text displayed in green with a dashed line underneath will display a definition for the term if you click on the word. Green text with a solid line underneath will jump to a new help screen.

(5) Click **Display** to see the Topics Found dialog box, where you will select the item that most closely represents what you are looking for.

(6) Click the **Display** button.

(7) This help dialog box is used to lead you to more specific options; click the **Create a new blank table** button.

(8) This dialog box has three types of help available: text, the green definition text, and buttons to go to another topic. Click the Close (X) button to close the help dialog box.

End Task

Task 9: Choosing an Office Assistant

The Office Assistant is a new form of interactive help that provides information based on what you ask. You can click the Office Assistant and type a question into the text box provided in the dialog balloon. The Office Assistant then searches for and displays several topics that might help you answer your question.

The Assistant can watch what you are doing and offer help with new tasks. It can also show daily tips. These tips change each time you start Access, or you can view and cycle through them as you want.

Right Click

Click

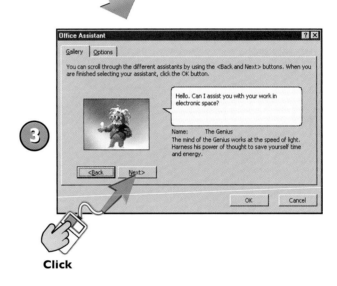

Click

1. Open the Office Assistant by pressing the FI key. Choose an Office Assistant by right-clicking Clippit.

2. Select **Choose Assistant** from the shortcut menu.

3. Click the **Next>** button to cycle through the various assistants, and then stop on the Office Assistant you want to select.

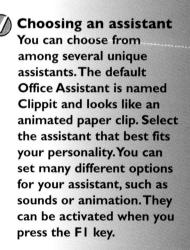

View assistants again
Click the **<Back** button to go back to an assistant you have already seen. Each assistant displays some of its characteristics as you view it.

Choosing an assistant
You can choose from among several unique assistants. The default Office Assistant is named Clippit and looks like an animated paper clip. Select the assistant that best fits your personality. You can set many different options for your assistant, such as sounds or animation. They can be activated when you press the F1 key.

(4) Click the **Options** tab when you have made your choice.

(5) Use the **Options** tab selections to customize your assistant by checking or unchecking the check boxes.

(6) Click **OK** after you have made all your selections.

Task 10: Asking a Question

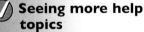

To use the interactive Office Assistant, you must ask it a question. It will then search through all the Access help topics and display a selection of topics that might bring you the answer you are searching for. The answers are shown in a dialog balloon, and when selected, display the help topic for that selection.

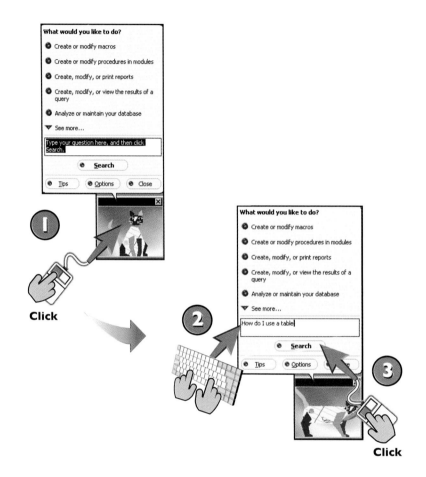

Click

Click

✓ Seeing more help topics

If none of the topics shown in the dialog balloon appear to be what you want, click the **See more** option to view more help topics. You can also try rewording your request and then click the **Search** button again.

① Click the Office Assistant's window and you will see the dialog balloon displayed above it.

② Type **How do I use a table** into the text box, or anything else that you want more information about.

③ Click the **Search** button to start the assistant searching for information.

Next Step

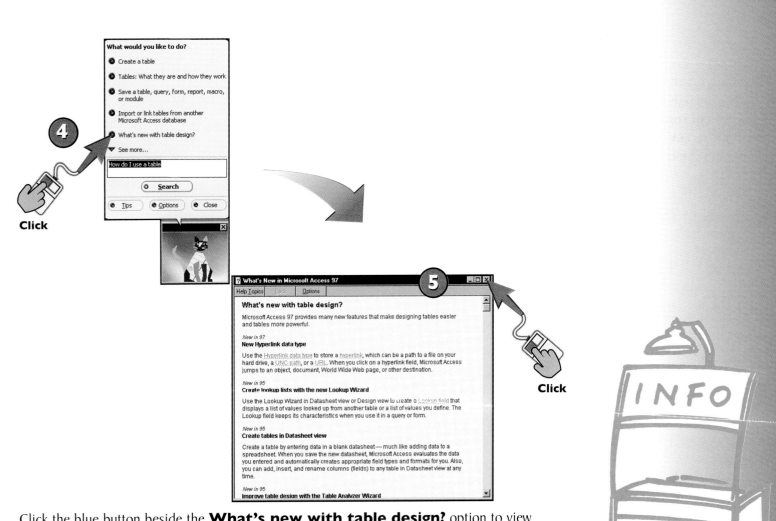

Click

Click

4   Click the blue button beside the **What's new with table design?** option to view the help dialog on this specific topic.

5   Click the Close (X) button at the upper-right corner of the help dialog box to close it and return to the Access desktop.

Task 11: Using Context-Sensitive Help

In addition to finding help by subjects and selected words, you can also get help relative to the specific task you are currently performing, or on a selected object. This type of help is called *context-sensitive help*.

For example, if you aren't sure what a specific object does, such as a toolbar button, or you simply want a better definition than a ToolTip, using the context-sensitive help option will display a pop-up definition of the selected object.

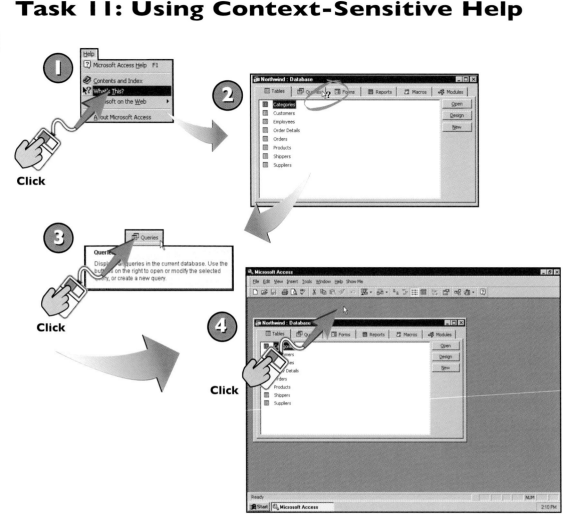

Click

Click

Click

✓ **The What's This pointer**
You can also display the What's This mouse pointer by pressing Shift+F1 from the keyboard.

Select the **Help** menu on the menu bar, then click the **What's This?** option from the drop-down menu list.

Move the mouse pointer, which has changed shape to an arrow with a question mark, onto the **Queries** tab button.

Click the **Queries** tab button and see the pop-up definition box displayed.

To get out of the What's This mode, simply move the mouse pointer to a blank area on the Access desktop and click.

End Task

Task 12: Exiting Access

Start Here

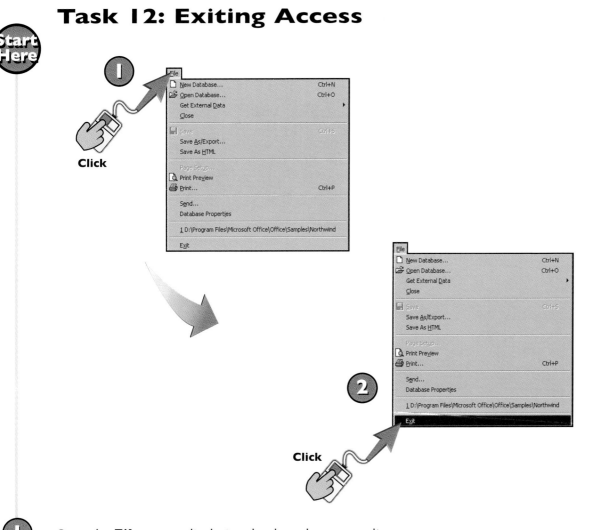

Click

Click

After you have completed your tasks in **Access**, or any time you leave your computer for a length of time, such as the end of the day, you should properly exit from the program. In the event of a power or hardware failure, this will increase your chances of a successful information recovery.

✓ **Exiting from Access**
You can also exit from Access by clicking the Close button (**X**) in the upper-right corner of the program window or by pressing the Alt+F4 key combination.

✓ **Escaping from a menu**
If after opening the File menu you decide that you are not ready to exit Access, simply press the Esc key to back out of the menu. You can also click the mouse anywhere on the desktop to close the menu.

1. Open the **File** menu, displaying the drop-down menu list.

2. Click the **Exit** command on the **File** menu and Access will shut down and return you to the Windows desktop.

End Task

Designing and Creating an Access Database

When you design an Access database you must understand all the components of one. All information is stored in a *table*, and each table should contain information about a particular thing: customers, products, orders, and so on. The table is composed of *rows* and *columns*—the rows contain *records* and the columns are *fields*. There is one record for each item in the table. Every record is divided into fields and every record uses the same fields. A field contains a distinct piece of information about the record. The goal of the relational database is to remove as much duplication of information as possible. Each table has information about one thing: customers, products, and so on. The records in a table can then be related to the records in another table through a *primary key* and *foreign key* relationship.

Tasks

Task 1: Adding a Folder for the Database

When you create a new database you must place it into a folder. You can add the new database file into whatever default folder Access selects, but you probably will want to choose your own folder.

It is highly recommended that you create a new folder for your Access databases. You can choose to place each database into its own folder or to group them according to types. Just be consistent in your choice.

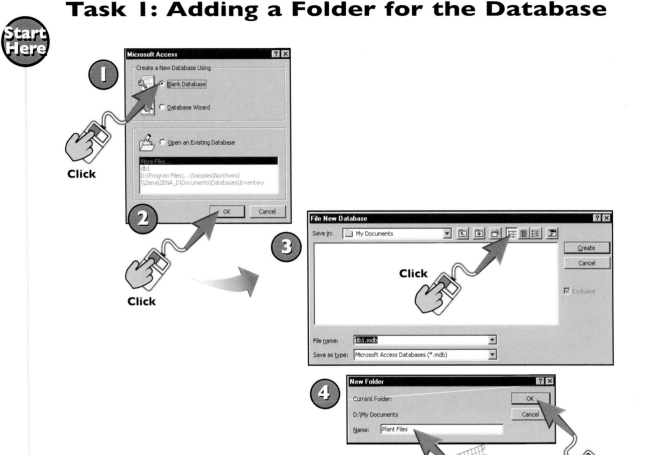

(1) Start the Access program and click the **Blank Database** option button.

(2) Click **OK** and open the File New Database dialog box.

(3) Click the Create New Folder button and display the New Folder dialog box.

(4) In the **Name** text box type **Plant Files** and then click **OK** to create the new folder.

Task 2: Creating a New Database

Start Here

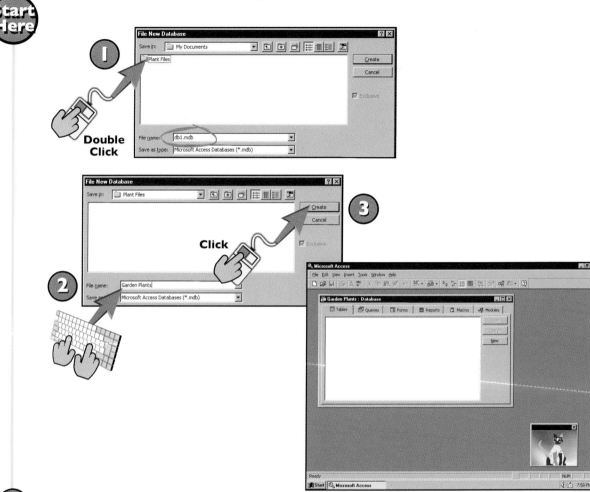

After you have created the folder into which you will place your new database, you must name the new database. Unlike most other programs, Access does not let you create a database and name it later.

Access automatically gives you a name for your database of *db1*. Unless you plan to create only a single database, you will want to give the file a name that is descriptive of its contents. The name you give is limited to 255 characters and can include spaces and most other characters. You can't use leading spaces, periods, exclamation points, the back-quote character, or square brackets.

1 Open the folder by double-clicking the **Plant Files** folder.

2 Press the Tab key once to select the old filename, and then type **Garden Plants** in its place.

3 Click the **Create** button.

End Task

Task 3: Using the Table Wizard

You have now created the file or document in which you will place your database and its tables, forms, and other objects. You have available a special helper called the Table Wizard that you can use to create many types of tables.

You will see a series of dialog boxes, and you simply must fill in the necessary information or choose different options. When you are finished, you have a new table.

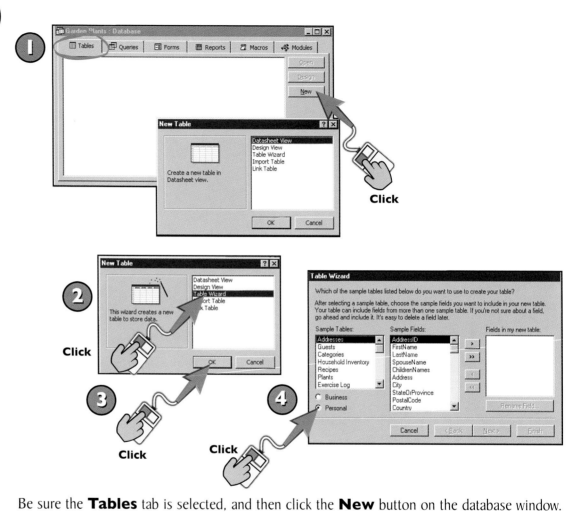

✓ **More samples are available**
Scroll up and down the **Sample Tables** list box to view the various tables available. Be sure to check out both the **Personal** and **Business** lists.

(1) Be sure the **Tables** tab is selected, and then click the **New** button on the database window.

(2) Click the **Table Wizard** option.

(3) Click the **OK** button.

(4) Click the **Personal** option button, and Access will display the list of personal categories of tables in the **Sample Tables** list box.

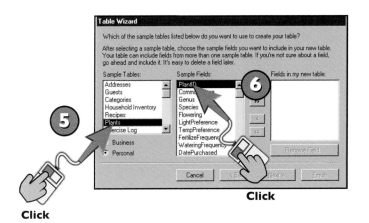

Click

Click

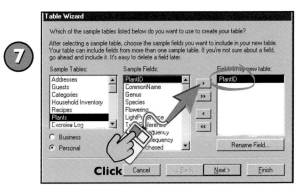

Click

5 Select the **Plants** table by scrolling down the **Sample Tables** list box. Notice the new list of predefined fields in the next list box.

6 Click the **PlantID** field in the **Sample Fields** list box as the first field to be included in the new table.

7 Click the **>** button and Access will copy the selected field to the list box on the right, where it will be included in the new table.

✔ **Need another field?**
If you do not see a field in the **Sample Fields** list box for the type of information you want to include in the table, don't worry. You can add the new field later.

Next Step

Using the Table Wizard Continued

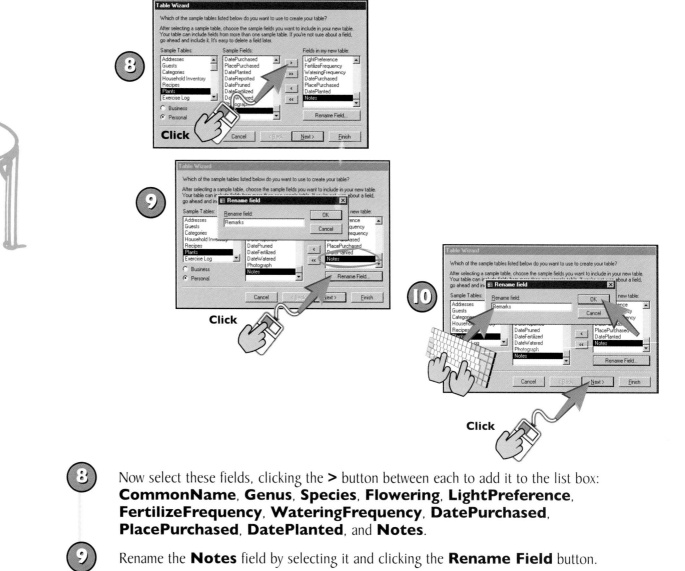

⑧ Now select these fields, clicking the **>** button between each to add it to the list box: **CommonName**, **Genus**, **Species**, **Flowering**, **LightPreference**, **FertilizeFrequency**, **WateringFrequency**, **DatePurchased**, **PlacePurchased**, **DatePlanted**, and **Notes**.

⑨ Rename the **Notes** field by selecting it and clicking the **Rename Field** button.

⑩ Type **Remarks** into the text box and click **OK**. Click the **Next>** button.

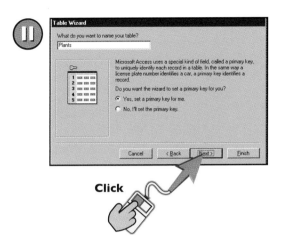

Click

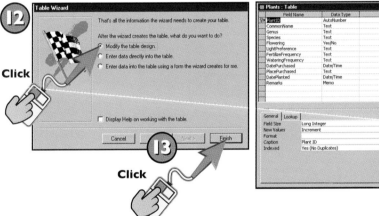

Click

Click

11. Here you enter a name for the database, and choose to allow Access to set a primary key. Click the **Next>** button.

12. This is the final wizard dialog box. Click the **Modify the table design** option button.

13. Click the **Finish** button and Access will complete the table and open it in the Design View window.

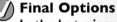 **Final Options**
In the last wizard screen, select the **Enter data directly into the table** option button if you want to begin entering data into the table. Use the **Enter data into the table using a form the wizard creates for me** option to allow the wizard to build a simple form you can use to enter data. Select the check box at the bottom to get help from the Office Assistant when doing the selected option.

Task 4: Adding a New Field in Design View

When you use the various wizards, there will be times when you want to make changes to the default settings. In the Plants table example, the predefined table does not have a field for the color of a flower.

To add a field to the table you must use the Design view option and add the field yourself. When adding a new field, you must provide a field name, a data type, and some formatting information.

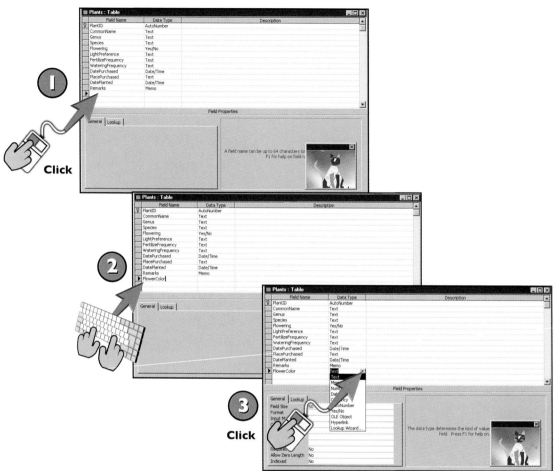

Click

Click

1 Click the mouse pointer in the first empty row in the **Field Name** column, just below the field named **Remarks**.

2 Type **FlowerColor** into the empty space.

3 Press the Tab key to move to the **Data Type** column and select **Text** as the data type. Click the down-arrow button to see the many other data types available on the drop-down menu.

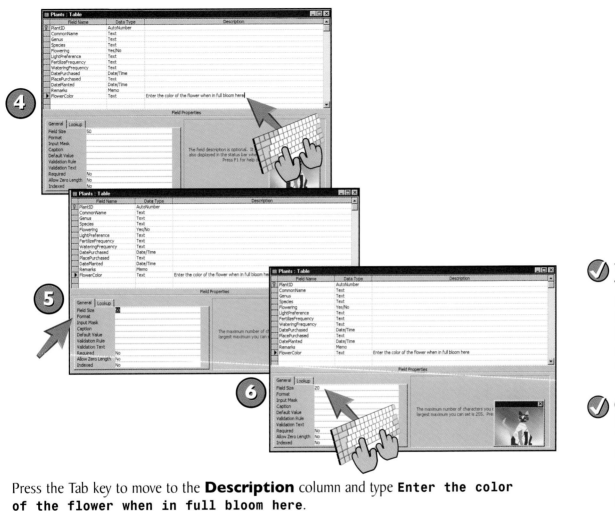

④ Press the Tab key to move to the **Description** column and type `Enter the color of the flower when in full bloom here`.

⑤ Press the F6 key to switch to the lower pane of the window.

⑥ Type `20` as the new field size for this column.

Task 5: Working with Number Fields

Number information is commonly used in databases because numeric data is everywhere. Numeric data includes things like quantities, pricing, cost data, temperature, and any other information stored as numbers. Access provides several special data types to handle number information only.

When you store number information in a numeric field, you can use that data in calculations. For example, you can multiply the price of an item by the number of items purchased and get the extended price. Calculated values are not normally stored in a database because they take up unnecessary disk space.

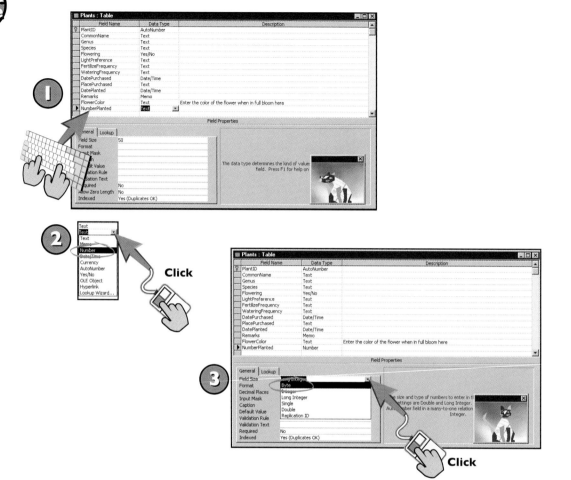

Click

Click

✓ Need help choosing a field size?

The Byte data type enables you to enter any positive whole number between 0 and 255. For help with the **Field Size** property press the F1 key.

Click in the blank row under **FlowerColor** and type **NumberPlanted**. Press the Tab key.

Click the button in the **Data Type** column and select **Number** for this field.

Press F6, or click in the text box beside **Field Size** and click the button to display the option list. Select the **Byte** option.

Next Step

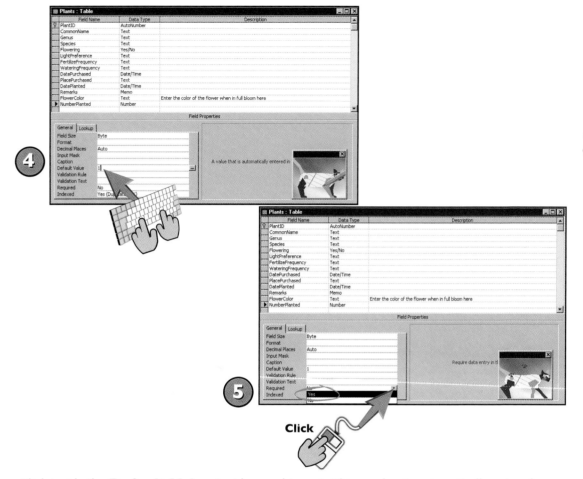

4 Click inside the **Default Value** text box and type **1**. This number is automatically entered into the field whenever you create a new record, but you can still enter a different number.

5 Move down to the **Required** text box, click the arrow button, and select **Yes**. This means that a value must be entered into this field, even if it is only a zero.

✓ **Using date/time fields**
For fields used for date or time information, select the **Date/Time** data type. A date field can hold any date from January 1, 100 to December 31, 9999.

Task 6: Adding a Yes/No Field

In some tables you will want to save data that can be a simple Yes or No answer. Instead of having to type Yes or No for every record, Access has the perfect way to deal with this information: the Yes/No data type.

Any field needing a Yes/No, True/False, or On/Off response can use this data type. The Yes/No data type can be represented in a table or form with a text box, a check box, or a drop-down list.

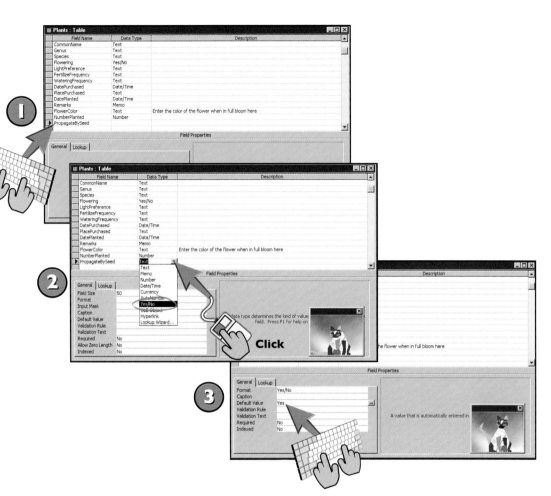

✓ **Reducing errors**
Using the Yes/No data type can help you eliminate data entry errors by enabling the user to select only one of two valid responses.

1 Move down to the next blank field row in the **Field Name** column and type `PropagateBySeed`.

2 Move to the **Data Type** column and select **Yes/No** from the drop-down list.

3 In the **Default Value** text box of the **Field Properties** pane type `Yes`.

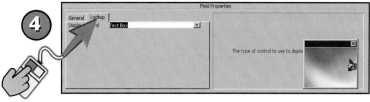

Click

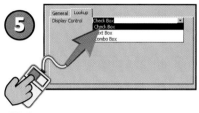

Click

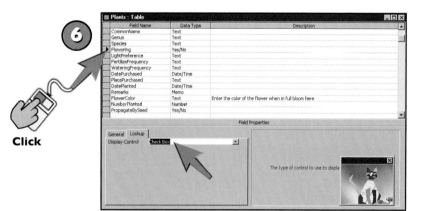

Click

4 Click the **Lookup** tab in the **Field Properties** pane.

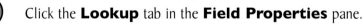
5 Select **Check Box** from the option list. A check box appears in both table and form views; checking the box is the same as saying Yes, removing a check is the same as saying No.

6 Click the **Flowering** field and change its **Display Control** from **Text Box** to **Check Box** for this Yes/No field.

 Shortcuts to data types
If you know the name of the data type you want to use, simply type the first letter and Access will fill in the type closest to your letter. For example, type the letter Y and Access will fill in Yes/No.

Task 7: Saving a New Table Definition

This table definition has already been saved once when the Table Wizard finished, but now that you have changed the table structure, you must save it again.

After you save the table structure, Access writes the new definition to your hard disk. This way all the new fields and properties you've just created will be there the next time you open the table.

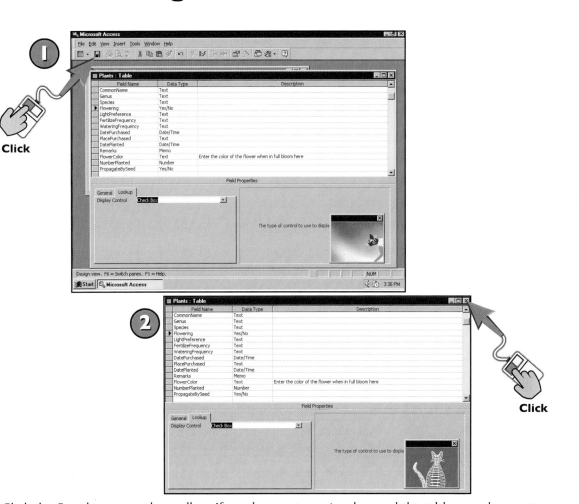

Click

Click

 Not yet finished?
If you are not finished with the new table, you can continue to add or change fields, and then simply save the revised table definition again.

Click the Save button on the toolbar. If you have not previously saved the table you also must name it.

When you are finished with the table and have saved it, click the Close (X) button at the upper-right corner of the table definition window.

Task 8: Opening a Table

Start Here

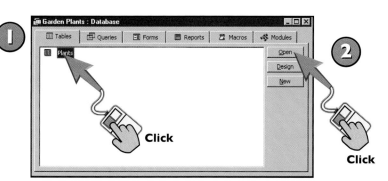

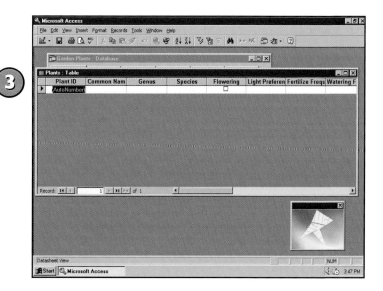

After you have created a table, you must open it in order to work with it, just like you opened the **Access** application to use the databases and table it contains. An unopened table is similar to an unopened ledger or order pad; you can't work with either one until you open it.

1. Select the **Plants** table by clicking it.

2. Open the table by clicking the **Open** button.

3. Now the Plants table appears in a datasheet view.

✓ **Other methods of opening a table**
You can also open the table by using the keyboard shortcut **Alt+O** or by double-clicking the table icon.

End Task

Task 9: Changing a Field Name

As you begin to work with a table, you might find that one or more of the field labels at the top of each column is not as descriptive as you might want it to be. Or even worse, you might find that you accidentally misspelled a label. You can easily change the field label.

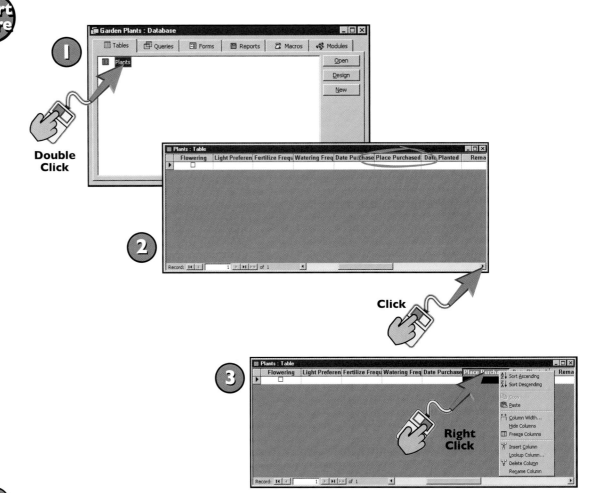

Double Click

Click

Right Click

 Working with scrollbars

If you scroll too far, simply click the left scrollbar button to bring the field back in view. It doesn't matter whether the field is in the middle of the window or on one side or the other.

 Open the **Plants** table by double-clicking it in the Database window.

Click the right scrollbar button at the bottom of the table window until the field column **Place Purchased** is displayed.

Move the mouse pointer to the column label and click the right mouse button to display the shortcut menu.

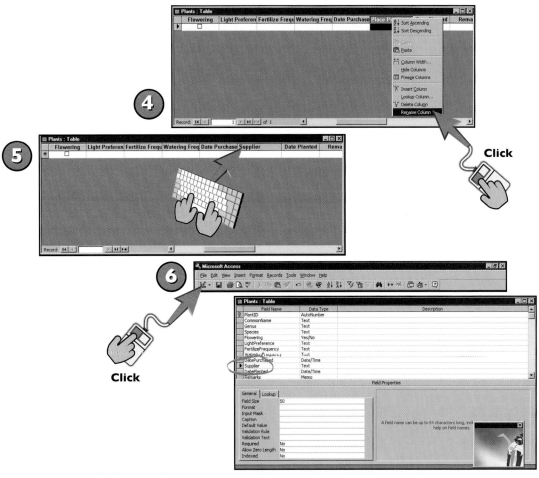

Click

Click

(4) Click **Rename Column** from the menu. This puts the field label in edit mode—see the blinking cursor at the beginning of the field name.

(5) Type **Supplier** as the new field label.

(6) Click the View button on the toolbar to see that the label has been changed there as well. Close the table; your changes are automatically saved.

✅ **Using shortcut menus**
Right-clicking the mouse will in most cases display a shortcut menu. The options on this menu will vary depending on what you are currently doing.

Task 10: Moving a Field Within a Table

Sometimes when you have worked with a table for a short time you will find that the fields are not in the right order. For example, you might input data from a handwritten form that includes a client's Social Security number, last name, and then first name. Your table shows the fields in first name, last name, and then Social Security number order.

This discrepancy between the written form and the table requires some fancy eyeball gymnastics that can get very tiring by the end of the day. Simply adjusting the order of the fields in a table takes just a few steps.

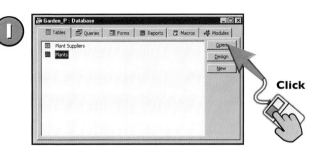

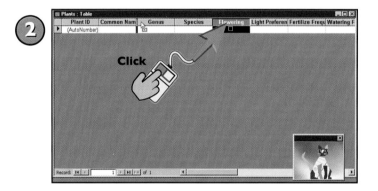

✅ **Table column order**
You can change the order of the columns in a table at any time. This does not affect any data in the table, column, or any other object that uses the column.

1 Open the Plants table.

2 Select the column header **Flowering** by clicking it once. See how Access highlights the entire column.

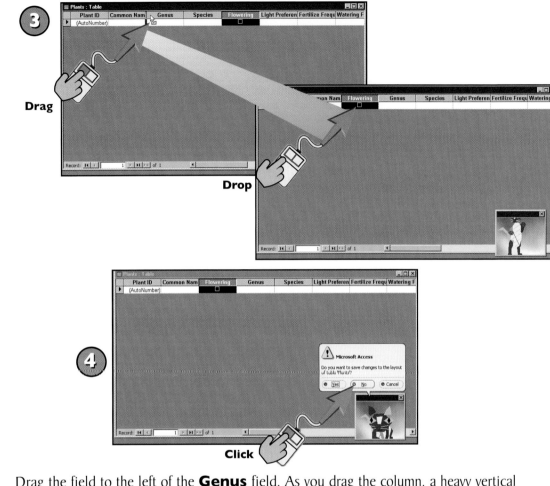

Drag

Drop

Click

(3) Drag the field to the left of the **Genus** field. As you drag the column, a heavy vertical bar indicates where the column will be placed when you let go of the mouse button.

(4) Clicking the Save button can save the new table definition, but we won't save this change. Click the Close (X) button and then the **No** button when prompted to save the table.

Task 11: Inserting a Field

As your business or needs change, you might find that not all the information you want is being captured in your table. In just a few seconds you can add a new field to an existing table.

It is best to make this decision as soon as possible, otherwise you will have to spend a great deal of time adding this information to existing records.

✓ **Where to insert a new row**
When you insert a new row, select the row that will be placed immediately below the newly inserted row.

✓ **Inserting several rows**
You can insert multiple rows by dragging down across as many selector buttons as you want new rows. The number of rows you select and highlight is the number of new rows that will be inserted.

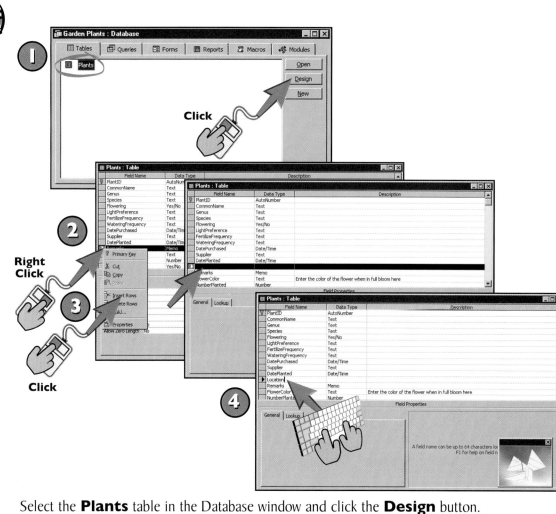

Click

Right Click

Click

① Select the **Plants** table in the Database window and click the **Design** button.

② Place the mouse pointer on the selector button for the **Remarks** field, and right-click to display the shortcut menu.

③ Choose the **Insert Rows** option, and Access will insert a blank line above the **Remarks** row. All other rows are moved down one place.

④ Type **Location** in the **Field Name** column of the new row.

Next Step

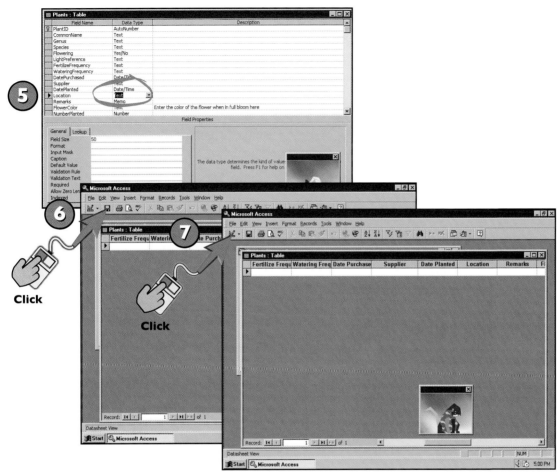

<table>
<tr><td>5</td><td>Press the Tab key and select Text for the data type.</td></tr>
<tr><td>6</td><td>Click the Save button to save the new table definition.</td></tr>
<tr><td>7</td><td>Click the View button to return to the Datasheet view.</td></tr>
</table>

 If you change your mind

If you decide that you do not want to save the new field, simply select **No** when prompted to save the table.

Task 12: Adding a New Field in Datasheet View

You can create a new field on the fly while working within the table. You don't have to stop and switch to Design view mode, add the new field, save the table, and then return to the Datasheet view.

You can quickly insert a new field into the table and begin adding information to it. The primary disadvantage is that you can't choose a data type or other properties for the field. The new field is inserted as a text field.

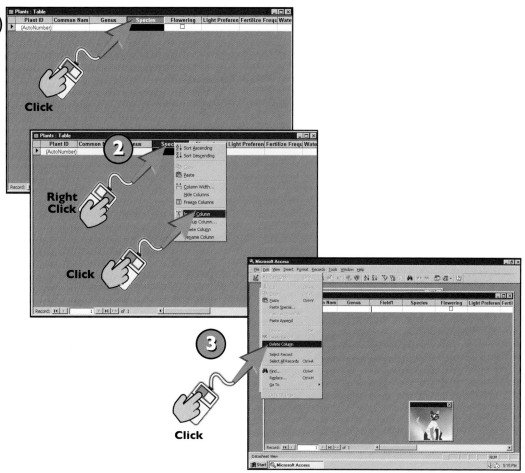

Click

Right Click

Click

Click

 Renaming a column
You have already learned to rename a column by selecting it and choosing the **Rename Column** option from the shortcut menu (see Part 2, Task 9, "Changing a Field Name").

Open the **Plants** table if it is not already open, and select the **Species** field label by clicking it.

Right-click the column label, and select **Insert Column** from the shortcut menu. Access inserts the generic field **Field1**.

We don't want to keep the column **Field1**, so select **Edit** from the menu and then **Delete Column**.

End Task

Task 13: Deleting a Field

As you begin to use a table in your everyday routine, you might find that there is one particular field that you never seem to use. If you find that a field is not being filled in, is never referred to in a report, or the information is also captured in another table, you can delete the field.

When you delete a field, all the information contained in it is also permanently deleted. You can't recover this information. In addition, any form or report that refers to the field must be corrected.

① Open the **Plants** table.

② Scroll through the table by using the right arrow on the scrollbar until you find the **Location** field. Select it by clicking the column label.

③ Right-click the label and select **Delete Column** from the menu. Access will delete the column from the table.

✓ Removing a column and its data
Be absolutely certain that you want to delete a column before doing so. You will not be able to recover the data when the column is gone.

Task 14: Building a Table from Scratch

The tables created with the Table Wizard don't always cover every situation. Using one of them might require you to revise the table, or you can create the table from scratch. By completely creating the table in Design view, you have complete control of the table definition.

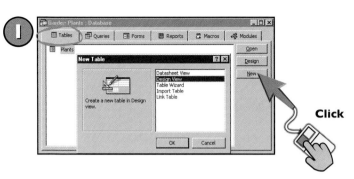

Click

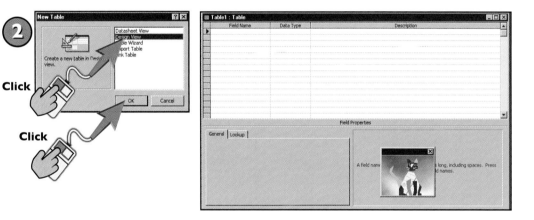

Click

Click

1. Be sure the **Tables** tab is selected, and then click the **New** button to display the New Table dialog box.

2. Choose the **Design View** option from the list and then click **OK**, opening a blank Design view window.

Next Step

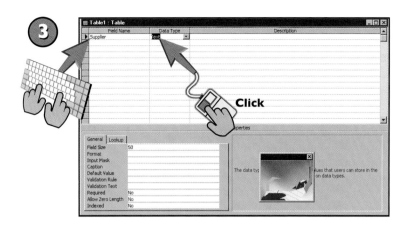

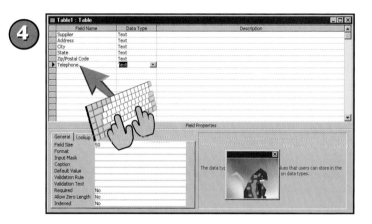

③ Type **Supplier** as the **Field Name**, and then select **Text** as the data type for the first row. This will become the primary key field for this table.

④ Add the following fields in this order: **Address**, **City**, **State**, **Zip/Postal Code**, **Telephone**. Use the default data type of **Text** for each.

✅ **Changing a field name**
If you notice a typo in one of your field names, simply select the name and retype it. Editing the field name does not affect any of the field properties that you have set.

Building a Table from Scratch Continued

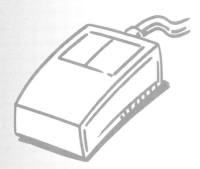

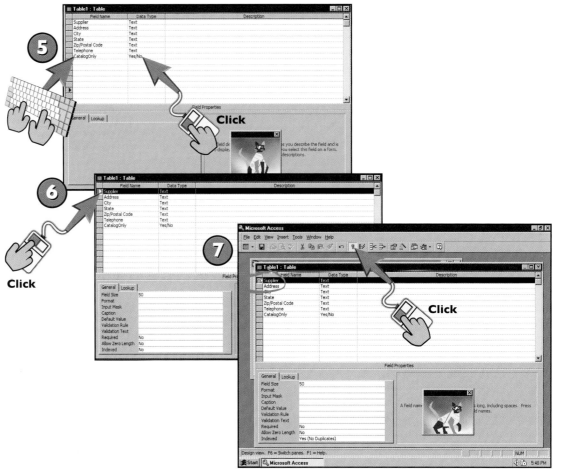

✓ **Clicking the wrong row**
If you miss with the mouse and choose the wrong row, just move the mouse and click again. The previously selected row will be unselected and the new row will be selected.

5 In the **Field Name** column of the next row, type **CatalogOnly** and select **Yes/No** as the data type.

6 Click the selector button for the **Supplier** row. This will highlight the entire row, ensuring you have selected the right row.

7 Click the Primary Key button on the toolbar. Notice the little key symbol now on the selector button.

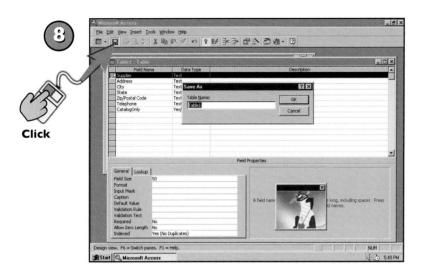

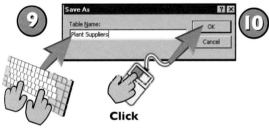

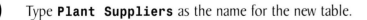

8 Now click the Save button on the toolbar.

9 Type **Plant Suppliers** as the name for the new table.

10 Click **OK** and the new table will be saved. You will now see it listed in the Database window when you click the Close (X) button.

Entering and Editing Data

After you have created the tables for your database, you can begin to enter information into them. Normally you will enter all the information for each record, and then move on to the next. You can think of each record as a single, blank sheet of paper. After you fill in the necessary information, you can turn to the next blank page and enter the next record.

With a database you can easily add new information to records and change information with just a few keystrokes. You can even hide selected fields of information from view. This is very helpful if you work with information of a sensitive nature. For example, if you have payroll records you can easily hide personal information before allowing another user to view the table.

In addition to being able to easily store large amounts of information, you can quickly find specific records by using the powerful Find command. You can also sort records by any field you choose.

In Task 1, "Entering New Information in a Table," you will need to enter the information contained in Tables 3.1 and 3.2 in Appendix A, "Tables."

Tasks

Task 1: Entering New Information in a Table

The reason for creating a database is to store information in a format that you can use. Access stores your information as individual records in the various tables you create.

When you fill out a paper form you are completing a record. Each block that you complete is a specific field, whether it is a name, address, date, or quantity.

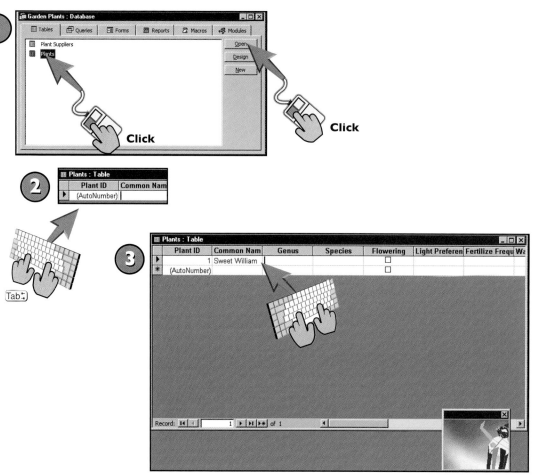

Start Here

Click

Click

Tab↹

 Autonumbering
The **Plant ID** field uses the AutoNumber data type and doesn't require or allow any input—this will be filled in by Access.

(1) Start Access, open the Garden Plants database, and then open the **Plants** table.

(2) Press the Tab key once to move the cursor from the **Plant ID** field to the **Common Name** field.

(3) Type **Sweet William** into the **Common Name** field, and then press the Tab key to move to the next field.

 Next Step

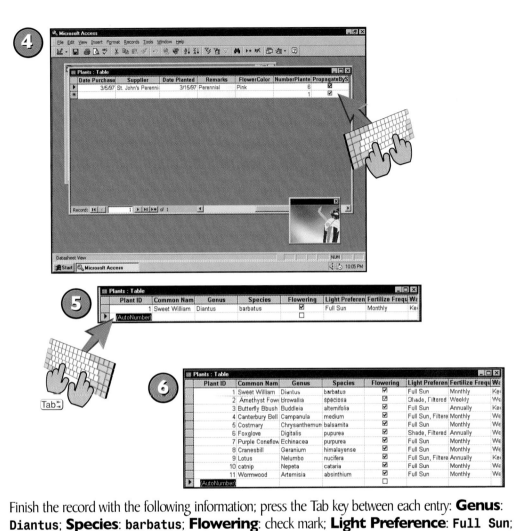

④ Finish the record with the following information; press the Tab key between each entry: **Genus**: Diantus; **Species**: barbatus; **Flowering**: check mark; **Light Preference**: Full Sun; **Fertilize Frequency**: Monthly; **Watering Frequency**: Keep Moist; **Date Purchased**: 3/5/97; **Supplier**: St. John's Perennials; **Date Planted**: 3/15/97; **Remarks**: Perennial; **FlowerColor**: Pink; NumberPlanted: 6; **PropagateBySeed**: check mark.

⑤ Press the Tab key again. Access automatically saves the new record when you leave the last field.

⑥ Complete the table using the information contained in Tables 3.1 and 3.2, repeating steps 2 through 5 for each record. Close the table when you are finished.

 Using check boxes
You also can fill in a check box by pressing the spacebar on your keyboard.

 Changing information
If you make a mistake when entering information into a field, simply press Shift+Tab to move back a field, and then retype.

 End Task

Some information that you enter in your tables for one record will be duplicated in another record, such as the same city or the same state. Even when every record taken as a whole is unique, there can be much repetitive data.

There are several techniques you can use when entering or editing information that allow you to copy data from one field to another without having to retype it each time. This can save you much valuable time and help to eliminate errors from mistyping information.

Task 2: Copying Information from Another Record

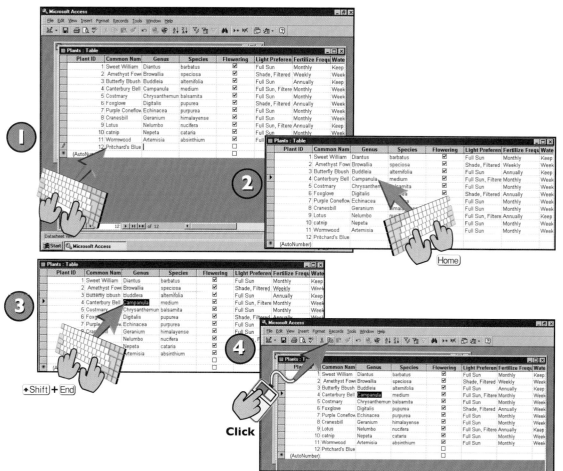

1 Open the Plants table, place the mouse pointer in the blank field at the bottom of the **Common Name** column, and click once. Type **Pritchard's Blue** and press the Tab key.

2 Move the mouse and click in the **Genus** field of **Canterbury Bell**, and press the Home key to move the insertion point to the beginning of the word **Campanula**.

3 Press and hold the Shift key and then press the End key, selecting the entire word, and then let both keys go.

4 Copy the selected text to the Clipboard by clicking the Copy button on the toolbar.

Plants : Table

Plant ID	Common Nam	Genus	Species	Flowering	Light Preferen	Fertilize Frequ	Wate
1	Sweet William	Diantus	barbatus	☑	Full Sun	Monthly	Keep
2	Amethyst Fowi	Browallia	speciosa	☑	Shade, Filtered	Weekly	Week
3	Butterfly Bbush	Buddleia	alternifolia	☑	Full Sun	Annually	Keep
4	Canterbury Bell	Campanula	medium	☑	Full Sun, Filtere	Monthly	Week
5	Costmary	Chrysanthemum	balsamita	☑	Full Sun	Monthly	Week
6	Foxglove	Digitalis	pupurea	☑	Shade, Filtered	Annually	Week
7	Purple Coneflow	Echinacea	purpurea	☑	Full Sun	Monthly	Week
8	Cranesbill	Geranium	himalayense	☑	Full Sun	Monthly	Week
9	Lotus	Nelumbo	nucifera	☑	Full Sun, Filtere	Annually	Keep
10	catnip	Nepeta	cataria	☑	Full Sun	Monthly	Week
11	Wormwood	Artemisia	absinthium	☑	Full Sun	Monthly	Week
12	Pritchard's Blue	Campanula		☐			
(AutoNumber)				☐			

Click

6 Microsoft Access

File Edit View Insert Format Records Tools Window Help

Plants : Table

Plant ID	Common Nam	Genus	Species	Flowering	Light Preferen	Fertilize Frequ	Wate
1	Sweet William	Diantus	barbatus	☑	Full Sun	Monthly	Keep
2	Amethyst Fowi	Browallia	speciosa	☑	Shade, Filtered	Weekly	Week
3	Butterfly Bbush	Buddleia	alternifolia	☑	Full Sun	Annually	Keep
4	Canterbury Bell	Campanula	medium	☑	Full Sun, Filtere	Monthly	Week
5	Costmary	Chrysanthemum	balsamita	☑	Full Sun	Monthly	Week
6	Foxglove	Digitalis	pupurea	☑	Shade, Filtered	Annually	Week
7	Purple Coneflow	Echinacea	purpurea	☑	Full Sun	Monthly	Week
8	Cranesbill	Geranium	himalayense	☑	Full Sun	Monthly	Week
9	Lotus	Nelumbo	nucifera	☑	Full Sun, Filtere	Annually	Keep
10	catnip	Nepeta	cataria	☑	Full Sun	Monthly	Week
11	Wormwood	Artemisia	absinthium	☑	Full Sun	Monthly	Week
12	Pritchard's Blue	Campanula		☐			

Click

Plants : Table

Date Purchase	Supplier	Date Planted	Remarks	FlowerColor	NumberPlante	PropagateByS
3/5/97	St. John's Perenni	3/15/97	Perennial	Pink	6	☑
3/1/98	Portland Plants	3/2/98	Annual, may be	Blue	6	☑
5/15/95	Portland Plants	5/20/95	Perennial	Blue	2	☑
12/10/96	Nichol's Plants & !	2/1/96	Biennial	Blue, Pink, Whi	15	☐
3/15/97	NW Hardy Plants	3/15/97	Perennial		3	☐
5/1/94	N/A	6/1/94	Biennial, perenn	Purple	12	☑
3/1/96	Portland Plants	3/2/96	Perennial	Purple	3	☑
6/1/97	St. John's Perenni	6/1/97	Perennial	Lilac	2	☑
3/15/97	Portland Pond's	3/15/97	Perennial	Pink	2	☐
6/1/95	St. John's Perenni	6/3/95	Perennial	White	6	☑
4/15/96	St. John's Perenni	4/20/96	Perennial	Yellow	1	☑
4/1/97	St. John's Perenni	4/1/97	Perennial	Blue	3	☑
					1	☑

NUM 7.42 PM

5 Click the mouse inside the empty **Genus** field of the new record.

6 Click the **Paste** button.

7 Enter the remaining information: **Species**: lactiflora; **Flowering**: check mark; **Light Preference**: Shade; **Fertilize Frequency**: Monthly; **Watering Frequency**: Keep Moist; **Date Purchased**: 4/1/97; **Supplier**: St. John's Perennials; **Date Planted**: 4/1/97; **Remarks**: Perennial; **FlowerColor**: Blue; **NumberPlanted**: 3, and **PropagateBySeed**: check mark.

✓ **Copy shortcuts**
To copy the contents of the cell directly above another, simply press the keyboard shortcut Ctrl+' (the Ctrl key plus the quote mark key).

End Task

Task 3: Editing Data in a Field

Start Here

In most databases you will create and use, the information is not static; it changes over time. Companies or people move and change their phone numbers, the number of plants you have increases or decreases, or you might need to correct a misspelling of a name.

Any of these things will cause you to edit or update a record in a table. Editing information can include correcting an erroneous entry, adding data to a record, deleting a record, or any other change necessary to keep your information accurate.

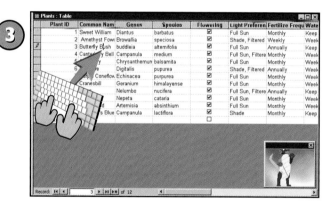

Click

Click

① Click in the field with the entry **Butterfly Bbush**—needless to say, the word "bush" shouldn't have two b's in it.

② Place the insertion point between the two b's in **Bbush**.

③ Press the Delete key once, deleting the single b to the right of the insertion point.

Next Step

4 Press the Tab key once, moving to the **Genus** field of the same record, and press F2. The insertion point displays at the right end of the entry.

5 Press the Home key, and then the Delete key to delete the small b, and press B to correct the entry.

Deleting on the left
Use the Backspace key to delete text to the left of the insertion point.

Switch from navigating to editing
The F2 key is a toggle between edit and navigation modes. In navigation mode the arrow keys move you from cell to cell, while in edit mode the right and left arrows move you within the cell entry.

Data you can't edit
Information can be edited in most cells at any time. You can't edit or enter a value in an **AutoNumber** field.

Task 4: Undoing an Edit

Sometimes as you are making changes to a record you will find that you accidentally made a change to a field in the wrong record. Access enables you to undo many changes you make to the information in a record as long as you have not yet moved from the field or the record.

After you move from a field you can undo all the changes to the current record, but not just to a specific field. After you leave the record and begin work in another, you can't undo any of the previous edits. You must retype the data.

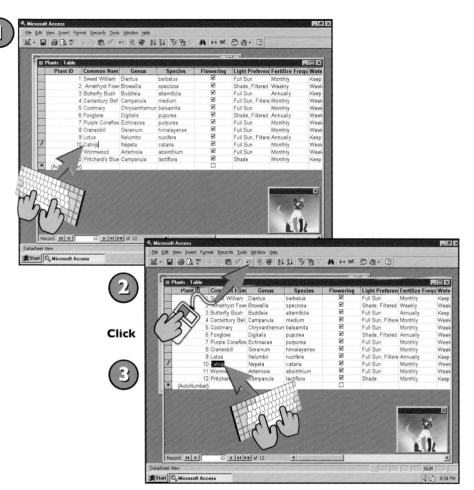

Click

✓ **Undoing an edit**
You can undo changes by selecting **Edit, Undo** from the menu. The **Undo** command itself will vary in wording depending on what you are currently doing.

Use the arrow keys to move to the **Catnip** entry in the **Common Name** column. This selects the entire value. Type **Catnip** to make this entry consistent with the others.

Click the Undo button on the toolbar and you will see that Access has reversed your edit.

Type **Catnip** once again, and press the Tab key to move to the next field.

Next Step

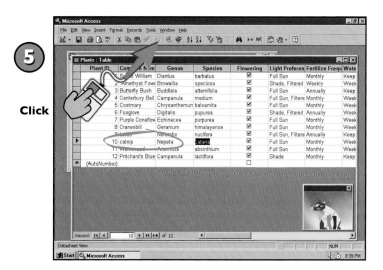

Click

④ Type **Nepetia**, a spelling you believe is correct.

⑤ Press Tab to move to the next field. You recheck a reference and decide that your original spelling was correct, so you decide to reverse all the changes you have made by clicking the Undo button again.

Task 5: Searching for Information

One of the most powerful features of a database is its capability to find information very quickly. How often have you needed to find information about a particular customer or product and not been able to find the information?

Access normally sorts records by the primary key field, but you can quickly search any field. In a table with many records, using the Find command is much easier than scrolling through the entire table.

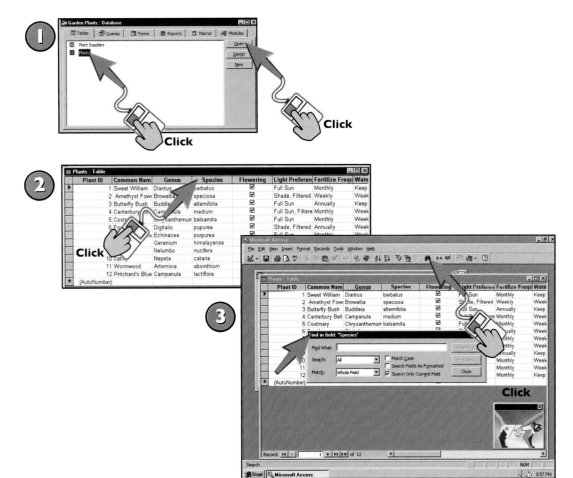

Open the **Plants** table.

Click the mouse pointer in the **Species** field of the first record.

Click the Find button on the toolbar. The Find dialog box displays.

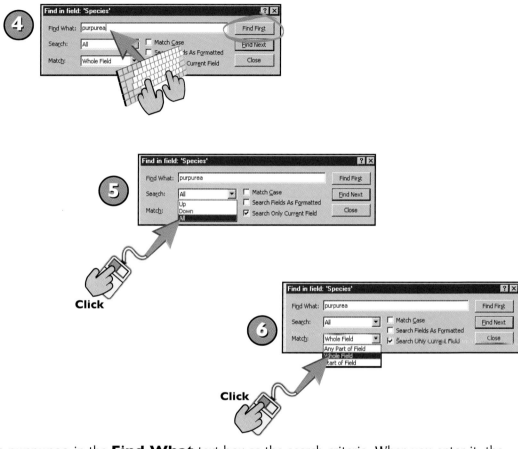

Click

Click

(4) Type **purpurea** in the **Find What** text box as the search criteria. When you enter it, the **Find First** button becomes active.

(5) If you aren't sure in which field the item you are looking for is located, select **All** from the **Search** combo box. You also have the option to search **Up** or **Down** the table from the cursor's current location.

(6) In the **Match** combo box, select **Whole Field**.

 Edit shortcuts
You can also use the keyboard shortcut **Ctrl+F** or the **Edit, Find** menu commands to open the Find dialog box.

Searching for Information Continued

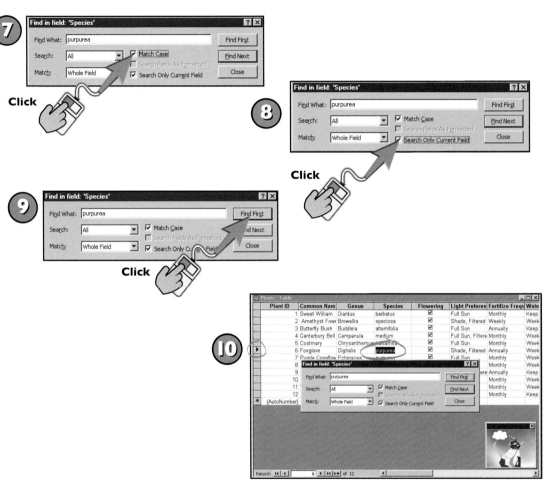

Click

Click

Click

Searching for partial matches
Access searches for exactly what you enter when the **Whole Field** option is selected. Use **Any Part of Field** to display an item that partially matches, or **Start of Field** to display those matches where the criteria is at the beginning of the field.

✓ **Match case**
When selected, Access will find only purpurea. When unselected, Access will find all matches, including purpurea, Purpurea, and PURPUREA.

⑦ Click the **Match Case** check box to select only those records that exactly match the value you entered in the **Find What** text box.

⑧ The **Search Only Current Field** option restricts Find to the current column. When unselected, Find will search the entire table.

⑨ Click the **Find First** button to begin searching. Access will highlight the first record that matches the search criteria.

⑩ When a match is found, Access moves the record selector indicator to the row.

Next Step

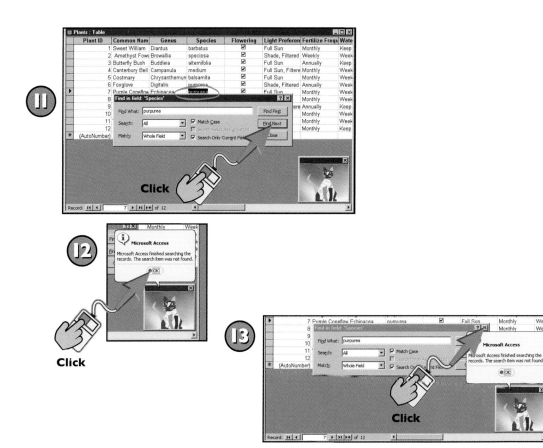

Click

Click

Click

Click

11 Click the **Find Next** button again to find any other records meeting your search criteria. When no other records are found, the Assistant will tell you so.

12 Click **OK** to close this dialog box.

13 Click the Close button.

✅ **Move the Find dialog box**
If necessary, drag the Find dialog box if it is preventing you from viewing the found record.

✅ **No match found?**
If you don't find any matches, try changing some of the search criteria and options in the Find dialog box.

End Task

Task 6: Replacing Selected Information

Start Here!

The **Replace** command not only lets you find information, but you can then automatically replace it with a new entry—all in just a few keystrokes and mouse clicks. Replace works very much like Find does, with a few more features.

Replace can be especially helpful if you accidentally misspell a city name throughout a table, or for example, when the phone company changes area codes.

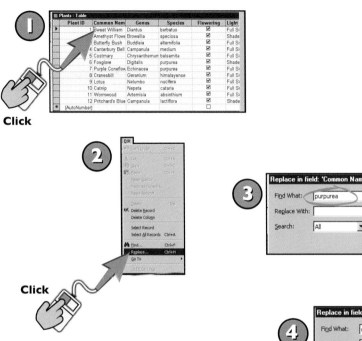

Click

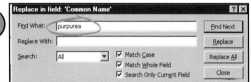

Click

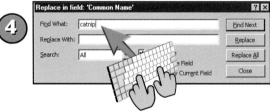

Click the mouse on the first record in the **Common Name** field.

Select **Edit**, **Replace** from the menu. Remember, you have not re-edited the entry for catnip.

The search criteria you used in Find is shown in the **Find What** text box. Access assumes that the last item you looked for is what you want to replace.

Click in the **Find What** text box and type `catnip`, overwriting the previous entry.

Next Step

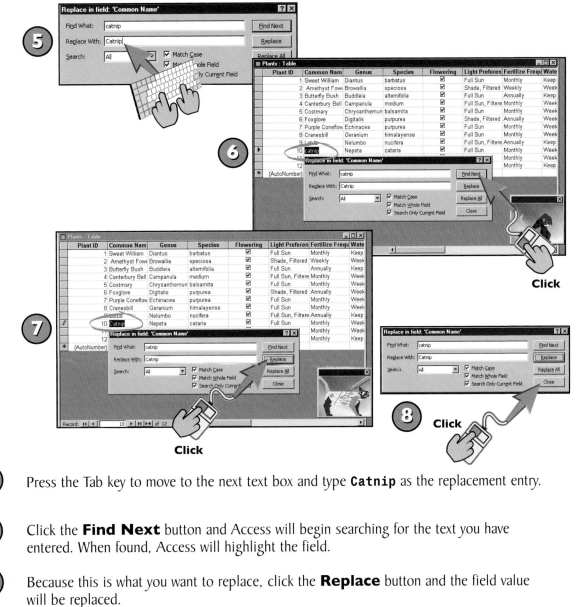

Click

Click

Click

5 Press the Tab key to move to the next text box and type **Catnip** as the replacement entry.

6 Click the **Find Next** button and Access will begin searching for the text you have entered. When found, Access will highlight the field.

7 Because this is what you want to replace, click the **Replace** button and the field value will be replaced.

8 Click the **Close** button.

 Replacing all at once
If you are sure that you want to replace all instances of the search criteria, use the **Replace All** button.

End
Task

Task 7: Sorting Records

From Access you can easily choose to sort the records in a table by any field you want. Often a table is sorted by a primary key field, which does not make searching for a group of records very easy. For example, you might want to temporarily sort a customer table by the State field, or you can sort the Plants table by the Common Name field. This is a much simpler way to scroll through your list of plants than in the normal order by PlantID.

✓ **Sort orders**
An ascending sort order looks like this: -1, 0, 1, 2, A, B, C, D,..., Z. Descending is in the opposite direction.

(1) Click the mouse anywhere in the **Common Name** column. It does not matter which record.

(2) Click the Sort Ascending button on the toolbar. You will now see the table resorted by this field.

(3) Click in the **Plant ID** column.

(4) Click the Sort Ascending button again. You will now see the table in its original order.

Task 8: Using Filters

Click & Drag

A *filter* is a special tool that you can use to display a subset of records from a table. You specify the criteria Access will use to select the records. Use a filter when you want to view or work with only a few records that have something in common.

For example, you can filter the Plants table to display all the plants that have blue flowers. In this task, we will filter for all plants whose common name begins with the letter **C**.

Click

Click

1. Place the mouse pointer on the left of the C in **Costmary** and drag across the C to select it.

2. Click the Filter By Selection button. You will now see only those plants that have common names beginning with the letter C.

3. Click the Remove Filter button to remove the filter and display all the records in the table.

✓ **Selecting with the keyboard**
If your mouse is giving you a hard time selecting a single letter, you can also select the letter by clicking to the left of it. Then press and hold the **Shift** key and press the right-arrow key once. This will select the letter.

Task 9: Filtering by Form

There is another method of filtering information, and that is by form. This is a more powerful method of filtering data, giving you much greater control over what records are displayed.

When filtering by form, you can use LIKE and AND operators to select ranges or similar records. These forms of criteria will be more fully covered later. For example, with filter by form you can view all plants whose common name begins with **C** and that require full sun.

① Open the Plants table and click the Filter by Form button.

② Click in the **Common Name** field and type **Like "c*"** as the first criteria. Access will filter for all records whose common name begins with C.

③ Click in the **Light Preference** field.

④ Click the arrow button to display the drop-down menu.

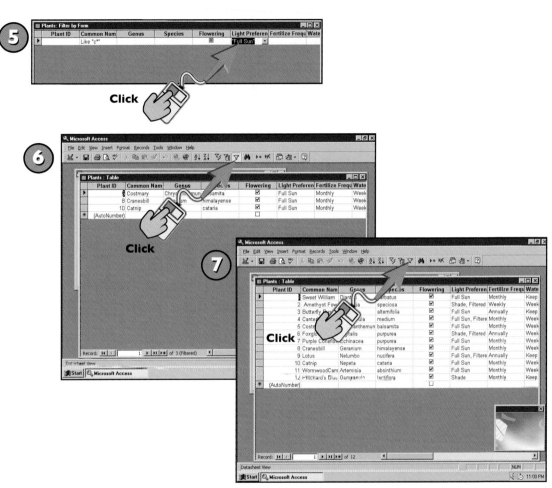

⑤ Select **"Full Sun"** from the list as the second criteria a record must meet before it will be filtered into our results set.

⑥ Display the results set for the filter by clicking the Apply Filter button.

⑦ Display all the table records by clicking the Remove Filter button.

✅ What happened to the filter button?

Notice that the **Apply Filter** button will move down the toolbar after you apply the filter, and that its name will change to **Remove Filter**. Same button, different function.

✅ Saving a filter

When you next close the Plants table, you'll be prompted by the Assistant to save the changes you have made to the table. The changes include the addition of a filter. If you say **Yes**, the filter will be saved with the table so that you can use it again.

Task 10: Deleting a Selected Record

One of the many normal maintenance functions of working with a database is that old, obsolete information must be weeded out or the table begins to take up disk space it doesn't really need. As records are added, you might find others that are unnecessary. For example, you might have records for a customer who no longer buys from you, or a discontinued inventory item, or in the case of the Plants table, an item you no longer grow.

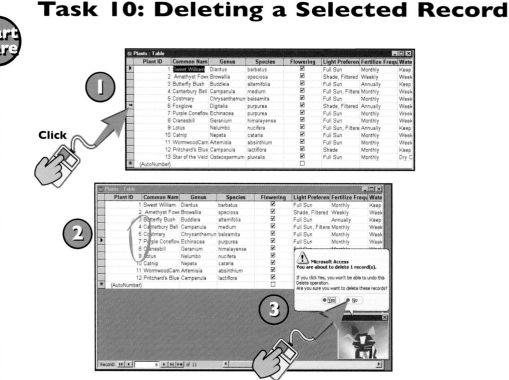

Click

Click

Other ways to delete a record

You can also use the **Edit, Cut** command on the menu, the **Cut** button on the toolbar, or the **Delete Record** option on the shortcut menu.

(1) Place the mouse pointer on the selector button for the plant **Foxglove**. Notice how the mouse pointer changes shape to a right-facing arrow. Click once.

(2) Press the Delete key and the **Foxglove** record is removed. The Assistant displays a balloon telling you that you are about to delete a record.

(3) Click the **No** option button, and the record is returned to its place. Clicking the **Yes** option will permanently delete the record.

End Task

Task 11: Completing the Supplier Table

Start Here

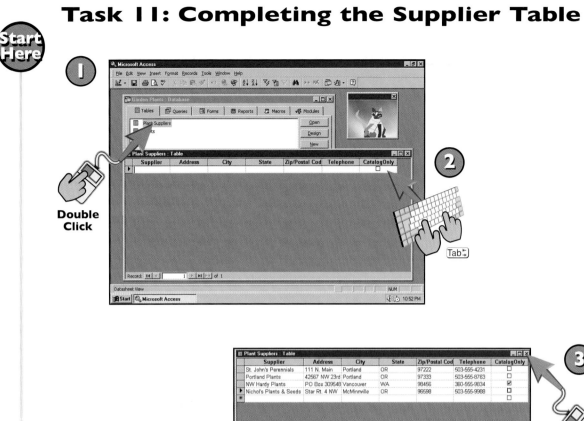

The Plant Suppliers table contains all the information about the suppliers from whom you have purchased plants. Use the techniques learned in Task 1 to enter the necessary information from Table 3.3 in Appendix A.

Double Click

Tab⁺

Click

① Open the **Plant Suppliers** table by double-clicking its icon in the Database window.

② Press the Tab key to move from field to field as you enter the information.

③ Close the table by clicking the Close (X) button.

End Task

Task 12: Resizing Rows and Columns

When Access creates a table, the row width and height are all the same. Although the height is usually fine for the standard font, the width might not be wide enough to display all the text. If the information contained in a field is too wide to be shown, only the data that will fit within the column is displayed.

You can easily expand or contract the width of a column or increase and decrease the row height. Changing the row height enables you to display the text of a field in two lines, add more whitespace between records, or show them in a larger font.

Click & Drag

Row and font size
Access doesn't automatically adjust the size of the font. If you decrease the row size too much, your records will appear to overlap one another.

1 Change the height of your rows by placing the mouse pointer between any two row selector buttons. See how the pointer changes shape.

2 Drag down to increase the row height. See the dark line extending from the mouse pointer across the table, indicating the size of the row.

3 Release the mouse button and see how all the rows in the table are now the new size.

Next Step

Plants : Table

Plant ID	Common Name	Genus	Species	Flowering	Light Preference	Fertilize Frequency	W
1	Sweet William	Diantus	barbatus	☑	Full Sun	Monthly	Ke
2	Amethyst Fower	Brow	speciosa	☑	Shade, Filtered Sun	Weekly	Wt
3	Butt...sh	Buddleia	alternifolia	☑	Full Sun	Annually	Ke
	Bell	Campanula	medium	☑	Full Sun, Filtered Sun	Monthly	Wt
5	...ary	Chrysanthemum	balsamita	☑	Full Sun	Monthly	Wt
6	Foxglove	Digitalis	purpurea	☑	Shade, Filtered Sun	Annually	Wt
7	Purple	Echinacea	purpurea	☑	Full Sun	Monthly	Wt

Click

Plants : Table

Plant ID	Common Name	Genus	Species	Flowering	Light Preference	Fertilize Frequency	W
1	Sweet William	Diantus	barbatus	☑	Full Sun	Monthly	Ke
2	Amethyst Fower	Browallia	speciosa	☑	Shade, Filtered Sun	Weekly	Wt
3	Butterfly Bush	Buddleia	alternifolia	☑	Full Sun	Annually	Ke
4	Canterbury Bell	Campanula	medium	☑	Full Sun, Filtered Sun	Monthly	Wt
5	Costmary	Chrysanthemum	balsamita	☑	Full Sun	Monthly	Wt
6	Foxglove	Digitalis	purpurea	☑	Shade, Filtered Sun	Annually	Wt
7	Purple Coneflower	Echinacea	urpurea	☑	Full Sun	Monthly	Wt
8	Cranesbill	Geranium	himalayense	☑	Full Sun	Monthly	Wt
9	Lotus	...mbo	nucifera				
		Nepeta	cataria	☑			
	...Ca	Artemisia	absinthium				

Record: 14 ◄ ► ►I ►* of 12

Click & Drag

Plants : Table

Plant ID	Common Name	Genus	Species	Flowering	Light Preference	Fertilize Frequency	V
1	Sweet William	Diantus	barbatus	☑	Full Sun	Monthly	K
2	Amethyst Fower	Browallia	speciosa	☑	Shade, Filtered Sun	Weekly	V
3	Butterfly Bush	Buddleia	alternifolia	☑	Full Sun	Annually	K
4	Canterbury Bell	Campanula	medium	☑	Full Sun, Filtered Sun	Monthly	V
5	Costmary	Chrysanthemum	balsamita	☑	Full Sun	Monthly	V
6	Foxglove	Digitalis	purpurea	☑	Shade, Filtered Sun	Annually	V
7	Purple Coneflower	Echinacea	purpurea	☑	Full Sun	Monthly	V
8	Cranesbill	Geranium	himalayense	☑	Full Sun	Monthly	
9	Lotus	Nelumbo	nucifera	☑	Full Sun, Filtered Sun	A	
10	Catnip	Nepeta	cataria	☑	Full Sun	N	
11	Wormwood Ca	Artemisia	absinthium		Full Sun		

Record: 14 ◄ 1 ► ►I ►* of 12

④ Chrysanthemum has dropped its last "m" into a second line. Move the mouse pointer to the dividing point between the **Genus** and **Species** columns; the pointer changes shape.

⑤ Drag the column to the right to increase the column width. Again, notice the solid line extending from the pointer.

⑥ When you release the mouse button, the column width is reset. Column width changes affect only the individual column. Close and do not save the revised table layout when prompted.

End Task

Task 13: Freezing and Unfreezing Columns

When you view or edit information in a table that stretches across many fields and several screen widths, the first few fields that identify each record usually scroll off the screen very quickly. When editing a certain record, it could be very easy to lose track of where you are in the table and accidentally edit the wrong record.

Access enables you to freeze selected columns so that they remain at the farthest-left position in the table at all times. This way the reference columns are always visible.

✓ Selecting several columns
You can also choose multiple adjacent columns by dragging across them.

✓ Freezing from the shortcut menu
If you are freezing a single column, you can right-click on the selected column and choose **Freeze Columns** from the shortcut menu.

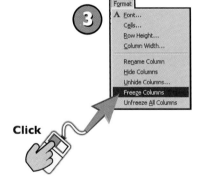

Click

↑Shift + →

Click

Place the mouse pointer on the **Genus** column selector, and when the pointer changes shape to a downward arrow, click to select the entire column.

Press the keyboard combination Shift+right-arrow to select the **Species** column also.

Select **Format** from the menu, and then select **Freeze Columns** from the drop-down menu.

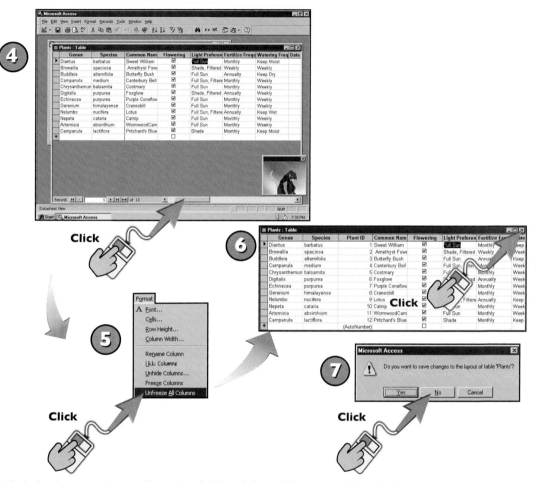

Click

Format
A Fo_nt...
C_ells...
_Row Height...
Column Width...

Re_name Column
_Hi_de Columns
_Unhide Columns...
_Freeze Columns
Unfree_ze All Columns

Click

Click

④ Click the horizontal scrollbar; the fields of the table move while the frozen **Genus** and **Species** columns remain fixed at the left side of the table.

⑤ Select **Format**, **Unfreeze All Columns** to unfreeze the columns, remove the solid dividing bar, and restore normal scrolling. This doesn't return any columns to their original places.

⑥ Click the Close (X) button.

⑦ Choose **No** when prompted to save the new table format. The next time you open the table it will be displayed in its original format.

✓ **Choosing columns to freeze**
You don't have to select the current leftmost column as one of those to freeze in place. You can choose any fields, but they must be adjacent to each other.

Page
81

Task 14: Hiding and Unhiding Columns

Many people work every day with sensitive, work-related information. When using such tables, you might want to hide from view those columns containing the sensitive data. For example, you might be helping a coworker gather statistical information about employee salaries, but you don't need to show them how much money a particular individual is paid. You can easily hide identifying information such as employee IDs and names.

Start Here

Click

Click

✓ **Hiding multiple columns**

You can hide any number of adjacent columns by dragging across all of them and selecting **Format, Hide Columns** from the menu.

1 Open the Plants table, and move the cursor to the column you want to hide—such as the **Species** column—and select it by clicking the column selector button.

2 Click **Format, Hide Columns**.

3 Access immediately hides the selected columns from view.

Next Step

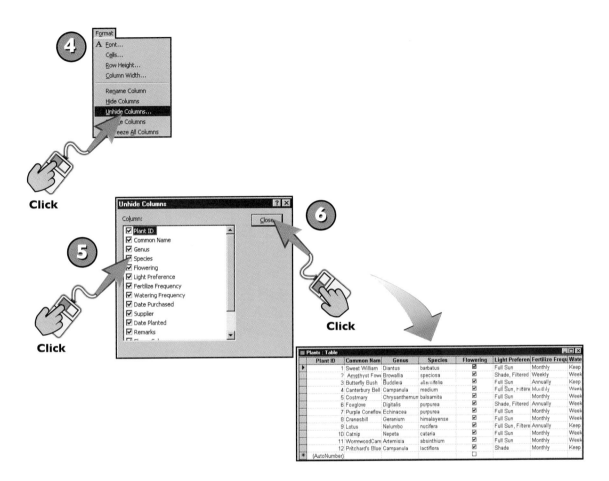

Click

Click

Click

Click

④ Unhide the columns by selecting **Format**, **Unhide Columns**. This displays the Unhide Columns dialog box.

⑤ The **Species** column, which is currently hidden, doesn't have a check mark in the box beside it. Click inside the box. The table blinks behind the dialog box as Access unhides the **Species** column.

⑥ Click the Close button to return to the table and see how the **Species** column is now displayed in its normal place.

✓ **Using Unhide Columns to hide columns**
You can use the Unhide Columns dialog box to hide columns that aren't adjacent to each other by selecting **Format**, **Unhide Columns** from the menu, and then removing the check marks for all columns you want to hide.

End Task

Using Database Forms

Forms are a more user-friendly way to view and input information into a database. Most of the forms that you will use are based on either a table or a query. They can be used to edit existing records, display calculated values, display information from multiple tables, or create a custom switchboard or dialog box.

Commonly, you will create forms that mimic a paper form that you currently are using. For example, you can easily create a sales order form that will enable you to enter an order directly into the computer. The form will also automatically fill in current prices and calculate totals.

Tasks

Task 1: Using an AutoForm

Start Here

You can quickly create a form from the currently selected or open object such as a table or query. With just the click of a button, Access will build a simple form based on this object. You can use the New Object button on the toolbar to create an AutoForm. Whenever you want to easily view records from a table without creating a new form, simply click the New Object button.

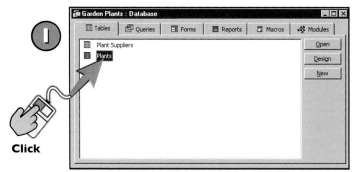

 The New Object button
If you opened the Plants table, continue to step 2. The New Object button works just as well on an open table.

1 Open the Garden Plants database and then select the Plants table by clicking on it once.

2 Click the down arrow of the New Object button and display the drop-down menu of options.

3 Select the **AutoForm** option.

Next Step

Click (at step 5)

Click (at step 4)

Click (at step 6)

4. When the AutoForm is displayed you can use the PageDown key or the record navigation buttons at the bottom of the form to view more records.

5. Click the Close (X) button.

6. Click the **No** button when prompted to save the form.

✓ **Using ToolTips**
If you place the mouse pointer on the **New Object** button and the ToolTip displays **New Object: AutoForm**, click the left side of the button to display the **AutoForm**.

End Task

Task 2: Building a Form with a Wizard

When you are ready to design a form with more features and controls than a simple AutoForm, try using the Form Wizard. This wizard helps you design a form with special backgrounds, colors, and customized fields and label styles.

The wizard guides you through a series of dialog boxes, each concerned with a different aspect of the form's design. When the wizard is finished, a complete form will be displayed based on your selections.

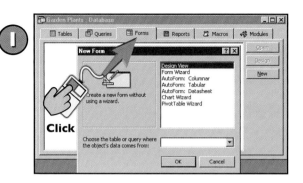

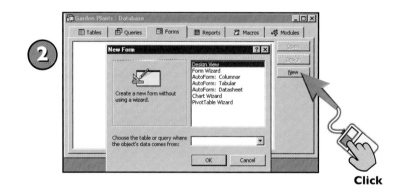

Saved forms appear on the Database window
Any new form that you create and save will be listed in this Database window, just as the tables you have created are shown in the Tables window.

Click the **Forms** tab on the Database window.

Click the **New** button or press Ctrl+N.

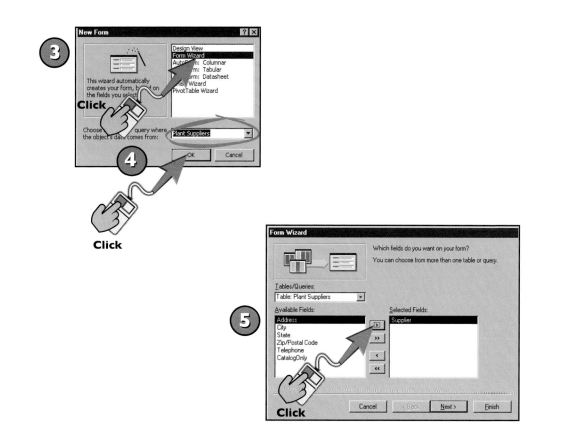

(3) From the New Form dialog box select the **Form Wizard** option.

(4) Using the combo box below, select **Plant Suppliers** and then click **OK**.

(5) Use the **Available Fields** list box to select the fields that will be included on your form. Select a field and click the **>** button to move the field to the **Selected Fields** list box.

Building a Form with a Wizard Continued

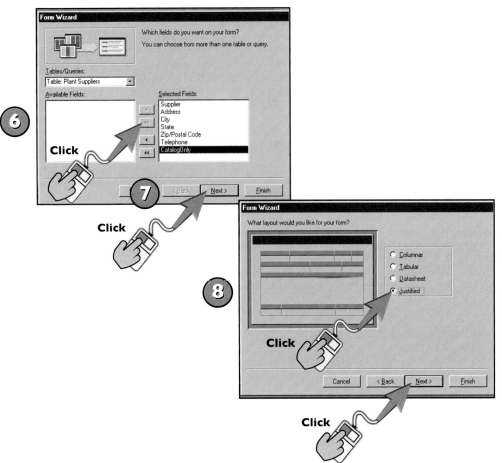

Next Step

✓ Removing a field selection
If you decide not to include a field, select it and then click the **<** button. Use the **<<** button to deselect all fields.

✓ Selecting a layout
Select one of the four layout options by clicking the layout option button; the thumbnail view will change as you click each option.

 Because you want to include all the fields from the Plant Suppliers table, click the **>>** button to include all the fields.

 Click the **Next>** button.

8 Select the **Justified** option and then click **Next>**.

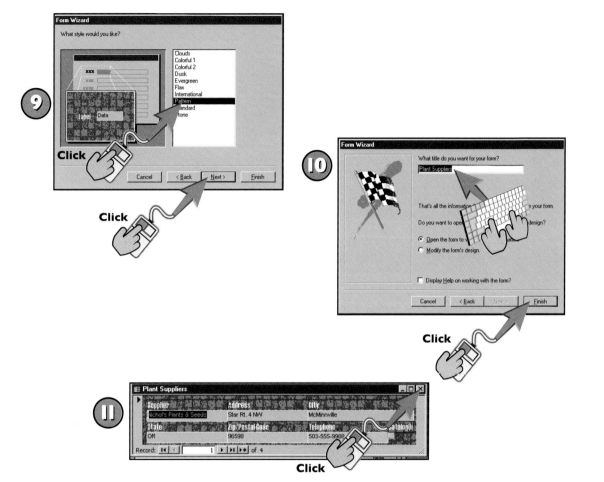

Select a style for the background, fields, and labels. Select the **Pattern** option, and then click **Next>**.

Enter a title for your form. The default name is the same as the object on which the form is based. Click **Finish** and Access will build the form.

You can now enter new records using the form, and they will be entered into the Plant Suppliers table. Click the Close (X) button.

✔ If you don't use a form
If you find that you don't use the form, you can always delete or revise it to make it more functional.

Task 3: Opening the Form Design View Window

Whenever you want to edit the design of an existing form or create a new form from scratch, you do so using the Form Design view window. From here you have the greatest control over all aspects of a form's design. You will be able to make all the decisions about the placement and appearance of fields, labels, and other objects.

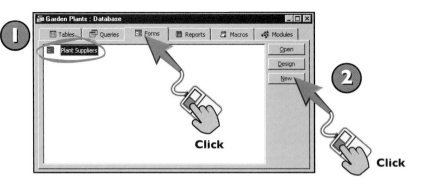

Click

Click

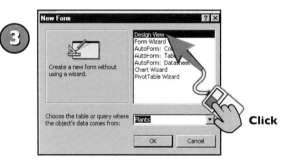

Click

① Click the **Forms** tab on the Database window. You will see the Plant Suppliers form that you just created.

② Click the **New** button.

③ On the New Form dialog box select **Design View** from the list.

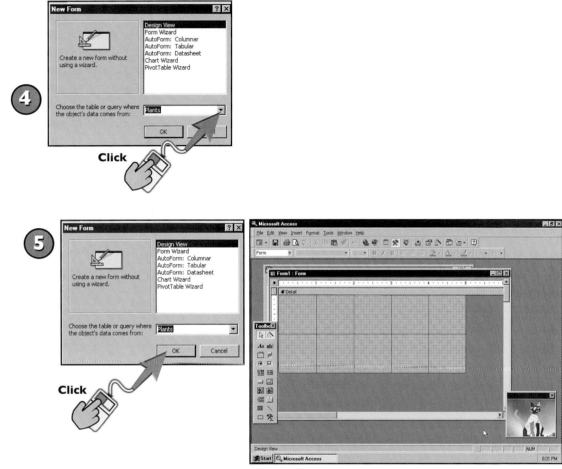

4 Choose **Plants** from the combo box as the base for the form.

5 Click **OK**, and the Form Design window displays.

✓ **Changing toolbars**
Notice that the Standard toolbar has now been replaced by two new toolbars: Form Design and Formatting. There is also a floating toolbox simply called Toolbox.

The primary purpose of creating a form is to simplify the viewing, adding, and editing of information contained in a table. This is done through the fields on the form, which are directly linked to the fields in the table.

Task 4: Adding Fields to a Form

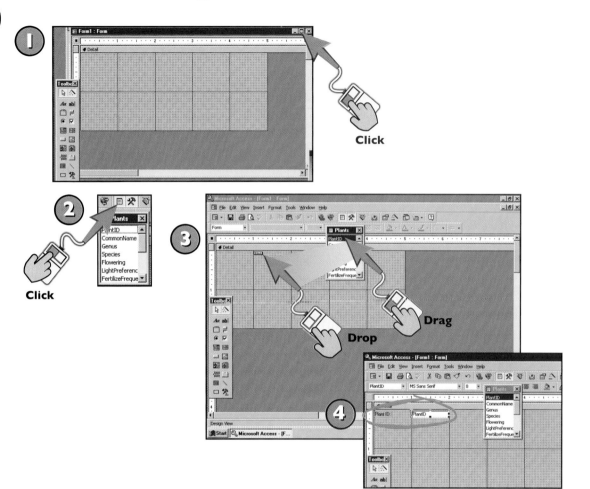

1. Maximize the Form Design window by clicking the Maximize button.

2. Click the Field List button on the toolbar. This displays a floating list box with the fields that are available from the object on which the form is based.

3. Click and drag the **PlantID** field from the Field List box to the Detail area of the form. The mouse pointer changes shape to represent a field.

4. Place the field beside the black one-inch grid line and drop the field by releasing the mouse button.

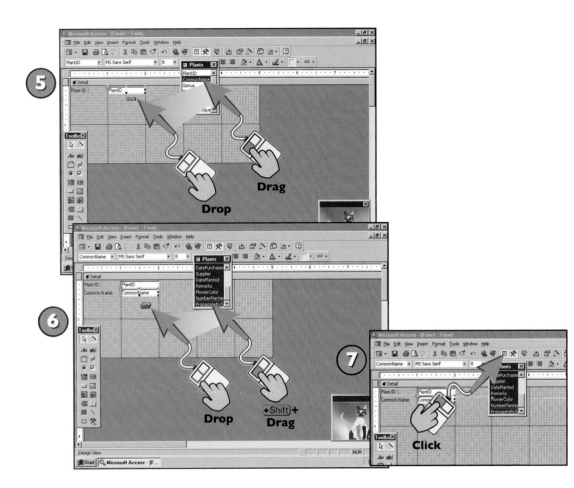

5 Select the **CommonName** field from the list box and drag it to the form Detail area underneath the one you just placed.

6 Select the remaining fields in the Field List box by clicking **Genus** and scrolling to the last field. Hold the Shift key while clicking the last field. Now drag and drop the group onto the form grid.

7 Close the Field List box by either clicking the Field List button or the Close (X) button on the Field List box.

✓ **Fields and labels**
When you place a field on the grid, you will actually see that two boxes are added. The right box is the actual field, while the one on the left is the field label.

✓ **Using the rulers**
Use the horizontal and vertical rulers to help you estimate the placement of the field.

Task 5: Moving Fields in Form Design

Unless you are extremely good at placing your fields in the right location every time, you will need to move some of them to different locations. This is especially true when you drag and drop multiple fields. These fields are placed in a simple columnar format, and you can get this same arrangement from the AutoForm.

Fields can be moved anywhere on the form grid. They can be moved with or independently of their labels, and they can be moved as a group. You also can adjust the size of a label or field.

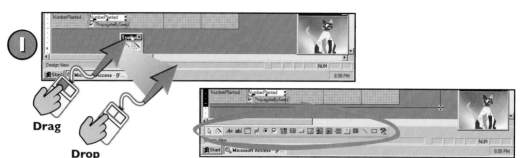

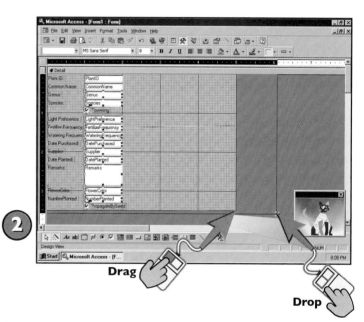

1 Click the title of the Toolbox and drag it to the bottom of your screen. The outline changes from vertical to horizontal; release it to dock at the bottom of the window.

2 Enlarge the form grid by dragging its bottom-right corner to the size that you want on the rulers. The mouse changes shape to a four-headed arrow.

Next
Step

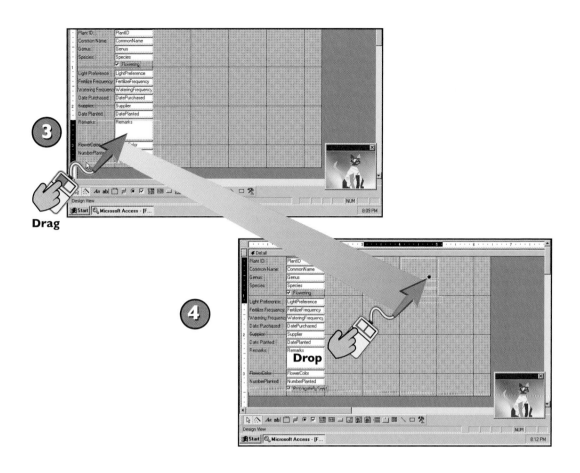

Drag

Drop

3 Select the last four fields and their labels by clicking the form grid near one of the fields and dragging a box around them.

4 Drag the group over to the right and top of the Detail area, and drop them.

✓ **The Check Box control**
Fields that use the Yes/No data type are displayed on the form with a Check Box control. You can change the formatting later if you want.

 Next Step

Page **97**

Moving Fields in Form Design Continued

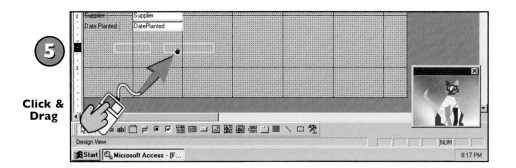

⑤ Click & Drag

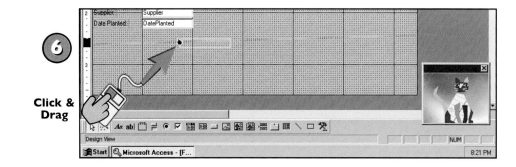

⑥ Click & Drag

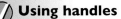

Using handles
Notice the eight black squares surrounding the field box. These are called *handles*. You can resize a field or label with these handles.

⑤ Move a single field by clicking and dragging it. Notice the mouse pointer again changes shape to an open hand.

⑥ Move an individual field or label by dragging the large handle in the upper-left corner. The mouse changes to a hand with a pointing finger.

Task 6: Headers and Footers

Start Here

①

View Insert Format Tools
- Design View
- Form View
- Datasheet View
- Properties
- Field List
- Tab Order...
- Code
- ✓ Ruler
- ✓ Grid
- Toolbox
- Page Header/Footer
- Form Header/Footer
- Toolbars

Click

②

View
- Design View
- Form View
- Datasheet View
- Properties
- Field List
- Tab Order...
- Code
- ✓ Ruler
- ✓ Grid
- Toolbox
- Page Header/Footer
- Form Header/Footer
- ...ars

Click

Microsoft Access - [Form1 : Form]

File Edit View Insert Format Tools Window Help

Form Header

Detail

Plant ID:	PlantID	Remarks	Remarks
Common Name:	CommonName		
Genus:	Genus		
Species:	Species	FlowerColor	FlowerColor
	✓ Flowering	NumberPlanted	NumberPlanted
Light Preference:	LightPreference		✓ PropagateBySeed
Fertilize Frequency:	FertilizeFrequency		
Watering Frequency:	WateringFrequency		
Date Purchased:	DatePurchased		
Supplier:	Supplier		
Date Planted:	DatePlanted		

Form Footer

Design View

Start Microsoft Access - [F...   8:36 PM

You use headers and footers to place information that is repeated only at the top and bottom of the form. A header area is often used to place information such as a title, a company logo, the date, and other information. The form footer area can be used for calculated fields like the total of an invoice and other summary information that you would often find at the bottom of a paper form.

① Select **View** from the menu.

② Choose the **Form Header/Footer** option from the menu. Two new grid sections are added to your form—the header at the top and the footer at the bottom.

End Task

Task 7: Creating Labels

Labels are used on forms for several reasons: as a title or subtitle, to give definition to different parts of a form, and to give instructions. You might have your own needs for adding labels to a form. They can help you give your form a more professional appearance, and they make your form easier to use.

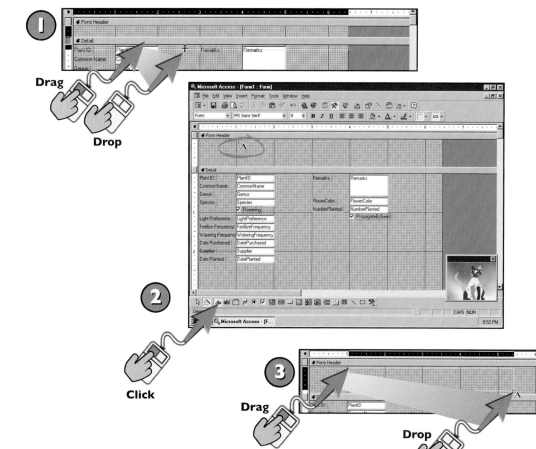

✓ Using the rulers to help with object placement
When you move or change an object's size, notice how a black band is displayed on both the vertical and horizontal rulers, indicating the current size and placement.

1. Increase the size of the header grid by clicking the top of the **Detail** bar and dragging down. The mouse changes shape to a horizontal bar with arrows.

2. Click the Label button on the toolbox at the bottom of the screen. The mouse changes shape to the letter A with a plus sign.

3. Drag a box. A blank label box is displayed with a blinking cursor inside.

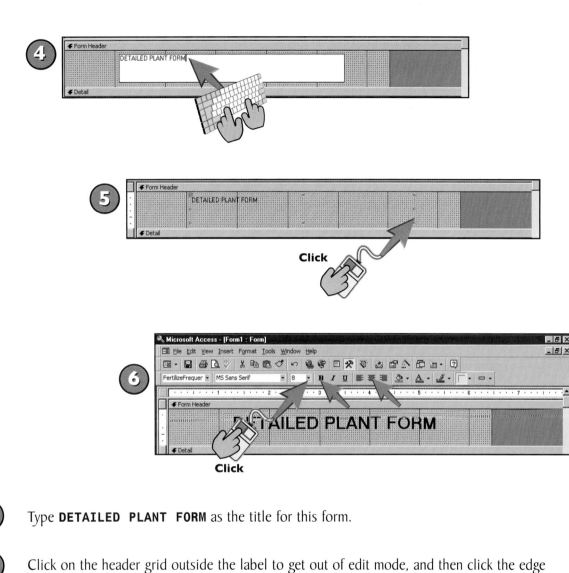

④ Type **DETAILED PLANT FORM** as the title for this form.

⑤ Click on the header grid outside the label to get out of edit mode, and then click the edge line of the label to select it.

⑥ On the toolbar click the Bold and Center buttons, and then change the font size from **8** to **24**.

✅ **Change a label's size with handles**
If the text doesn't fit inside your label, simply select it and use the handles to increase its size.

✅ **Unwanted label?**
If you decide that you don't need a label, simply select it and then press Delete.

The combo box is a versatile method of getting data into a form. You can restrict the choices a user has to only one of a list of options, or you can allow them to type something else. Combo boxes can help you ensure that your data is consistent for the most frequently used information, but still flexible enough to meet all your needs.

Information in a combo box can be based on a list of values you enter when you create the control, or on a query or table. If you must frequently update the choices displayed, base the control on a table or query. Changing this information is easier than changing the control list.

Task 8: Using a Combo Box

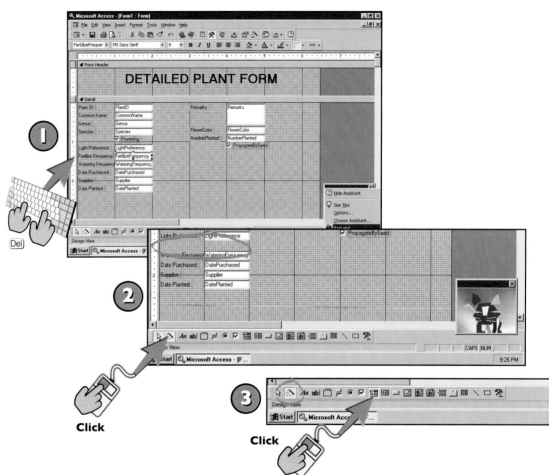

Click

Click

① Select the **FertilizeFrequency** field on your form and press the Delete key.

② The field is removed from your form, but the underlying table is not. Click the Control Wizards button on the toolbox.

③ Click the Combo Box button. Notice that the Control Wizards button remains depressed. It is used in combination with other buttons.

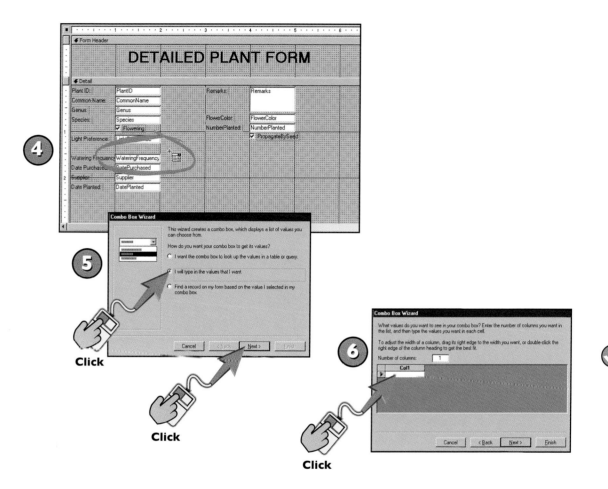

DETAILED PLANT FORM

Click

Click

Click

4. The mouse changes shape to a plus sign and a combo box. Place it where you want the new combo box placed on the form and click.

5. The first of several Combo Box Wizard dialog boxes displays. Click the second option button, and then click **Next>**.

6. Choose the number of columns for the combo box. The default is I, which is fine. Click in the Col1 field.

 Deleting a label doesn't delete the field
Remember, you must select the field, not its attached label. If you accidentally delete only the field label, the field will remain on the form. Simply select the field and delete it.

 The Back button
You can always use the Back button to return to a previous dialog box and change a setting.

Using a Combo Box Continued

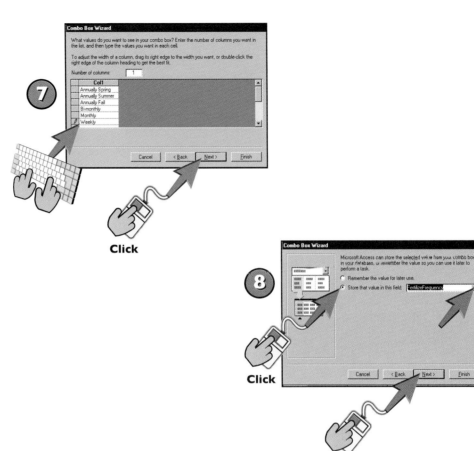

Click

Click

Click

 Choosing the number of columns
The number of columns displayed in the lower half of the dialog box depends on the number entered above.

⑦ Enter the following values; press Tab after each: **Annually Spring**, **Annually Summer**, **Annually Fall**, **Bi-monthly**, **Monthly**, and **Weekly**. Click **Next>** when finished.

⑧ Choose the second option button in this dialog box, and select **FertilizeFrequency** from the combo box. The values you select will be entered into this field in the table. Click **Next>**.

Next Step

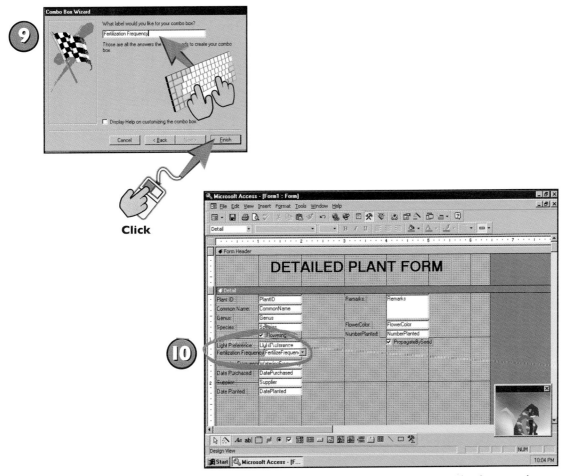

Click

9 Type **Fertilization Frequency** into the text box as the label for the combo box, and click the **Finish** button.

10 Adjust the label size for the combo box so you can read the entire label. You must move the combo box field over a little to accomplish this.

PART 4

Task 9: Adding a List Box

A list box is best used with a field in which you want to restrict a user to a very limited number of valid responses. The user does not have the option of entering a different response. A list box normally can take up more form space than other types of controls and fields.

Generally, limit a list box to no more than 10 responses. The list becomes crowded when you use more than that, and searching through it might take longer than typing an item.

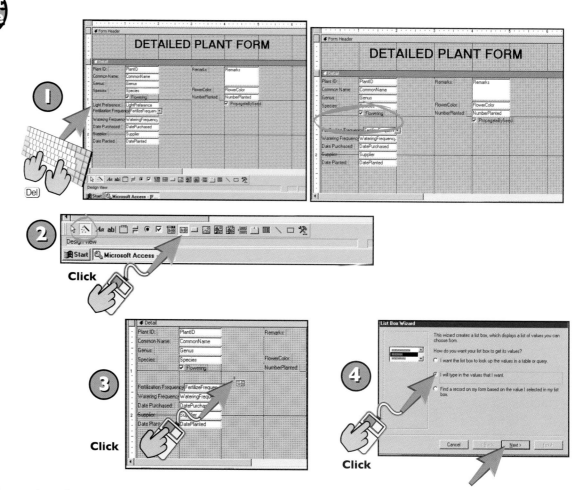

Start Here

Del

Click

Click

Click

Undoing an action
If you delete the wrong field, click the Undo button and Access will place the field back into position.

1 Select the **LightPreference** field and press the Delete key to remove the field and its attached label from the form.

2 Be sure the Control Wizards button is selected, and then click the List Box button on the toolbar.

3 Place the mouse, now in the shape of a plus sign and list box, at the place where you deleted the field and click once.

4 Click the second option button, and then click the **Next>** button.

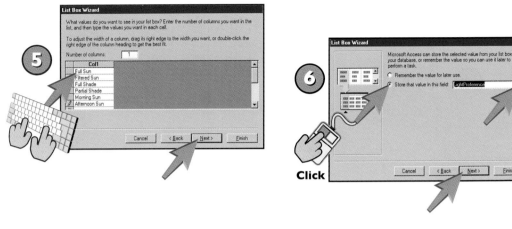

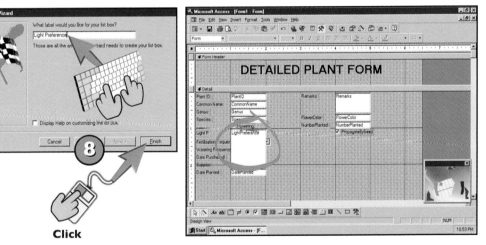

Click

Click

5. Type **Full Sun** into the first cell and press Tab. Fill this dialog box with the following values: **Filtered Sun**, **Full Shade**, **Partial Shade**, **Morning Sun**, **Afternoon Sun**. Click **Next>**.

6. Click the second option button, and select **LightPreference** in the combo box beside it. Click **Next>**.

7. Type **Light Preference** into the text box for the label.

8. Click the **Finish** button.

Task 10: Moving Objects

As the design of your form begins to take shape, you might find that some objects are not where they should be, or that another field's size must be increased or decreased, causing its neighbors to be out of place. Or in the case of our list box, it has covered several other fields.

You can move fields one at a time or as a group. Moving fields as a group gives you the advantage that they all remain in the same relative position to each other.

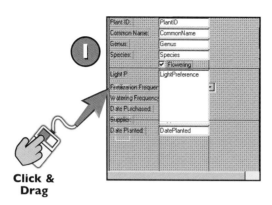

**Click &
Drag**

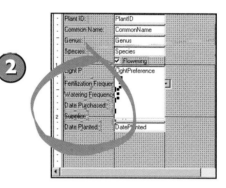

1 Place the mouse pointer on the form grid under the label **Date Planted** and drag up until the selection box touches the **Fertilization** label.

2 Release the mouse button and you will see that you have selected all the covered fields and their labels.

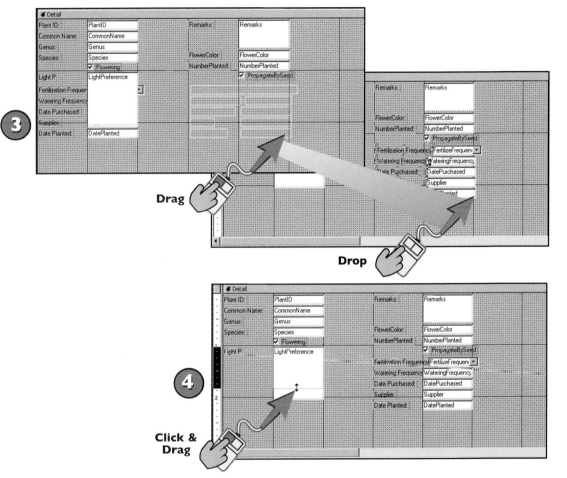

Drag

Drop

Click & Drag

(3) Drag these five fields and their labels to the right half of the form. Release the mouse button and the fields will be dropped in their new location.

(4) Select the **LightPreference** field and drag its bottom resize handle up until it is approximately 3/4-inch in height.

 If you miss a field
If you miss a field, just reselect the group and make the selection box larger.

 Alternative way to select objects
You can also select objects that aren't adjacent to each other by pressing and holding the Shift key while you click each object you want to move.

 Adjusting field positions
If your fields end up being slightly to one side or the other, just drag them back into place.

 End Task

Task 11: Editing a Label

As you continue to design your form, you might find that some of the default labels assigned to your fields don't adequately describe the information that should be entered. In order for your form to be of real use to its users, they should be able to know what information is required for a field simply by reading its label.

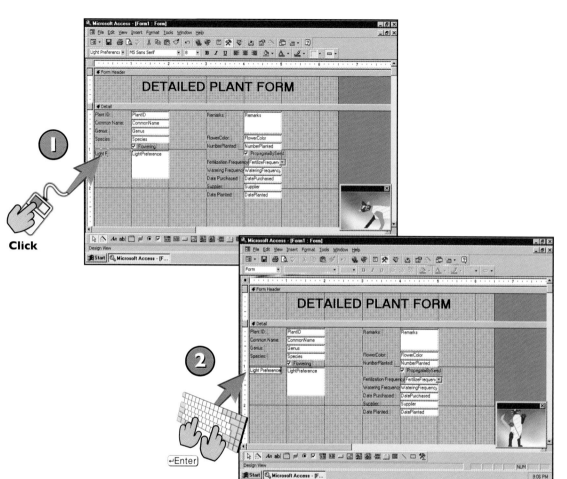

Click

 F2 and edit mode
You can also press the F2 key to switch into and out of edit mode.

Select the attached label for the **LightPreference** field, which now reads **Light P**.

Press the Enter key to switch to edit mode, placing the insertion point at the end of the label's text.

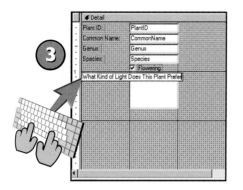

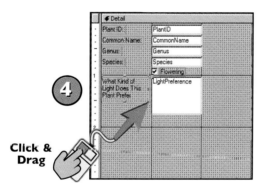

**Click &
Drag**

 Delete the existing label by pressing the Backspace key, and then type **What Kind of Light Does This Plant Prefer**. Press Enter again to toggle out of edit mode.

Select and drag the lower-right corner of the label. The label can now hold three lines of text.

Task 12: Using an Option Button

Several controls enable you to enter a Yes/No type of response: toggle buttons, option buttons, and check boxes. Option buttons and check boxes can be used in both forms and reports, whereas toggle buttons can be used only on forms. Each of these work in much the same way, so only option buttons are discussed here.

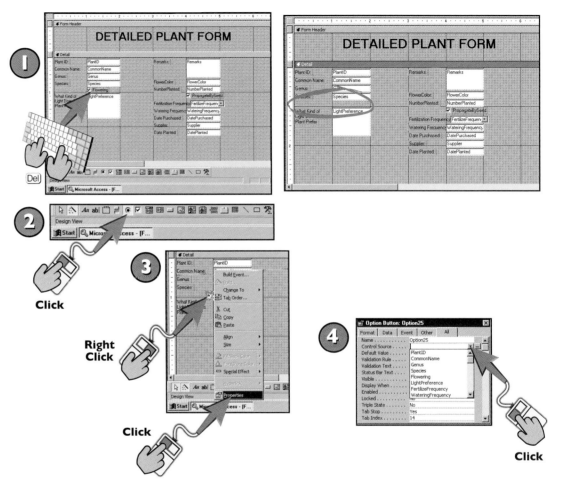

✓ **Open the Property sheet**
You can also open the property sheet by selecting the object and clicking the Properties button on the toolbar.

1. Select the **Flowering** field and press the Delete key to remove it from the form.

2. Click the Option Button tool on the toolbox, and move the mouse to the same place the **Flowering** field had been located.

3. Click once and an option button control is placed on your form. Right-click the option button and select **Properties** from the shortcut menu.

4. Press the down-arrow key to select the Control Source text box on the property sheet for the new control. Click the arrow button on the combo box to display the list of available field objects.

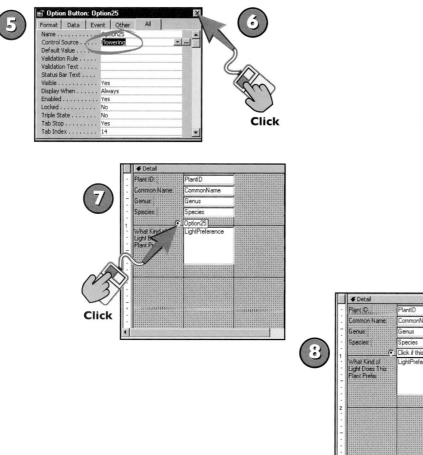

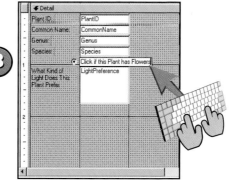

 Select **Flowering** from the list. This field controls this object button.

Close the property sheet by clicking its Close (X) button.

Select the label for the option button, and press the Enter key to switch to edit mode.

Delete the existing label and type **Click if this Plant has Flowers**. Press Enter again to switch out of edit mode.

✓ **Default flowering button**
When you click this button, Access enters Yes into this field in the Plants table.

Task 13: Adding a Calculated Field

You can use calculated fields for many different things. A calculated field can combine information from two or more fields into a single field. You can use a calculated field to perform arithmetic functions (add, subtract, multiply, and divide) between two fields such as a quantity and a price to give the extended price. You can also use a calculated field to sum a group of numbers and display the total.

In this example, you will create a calculated field that will sum the number of plants you have planted.

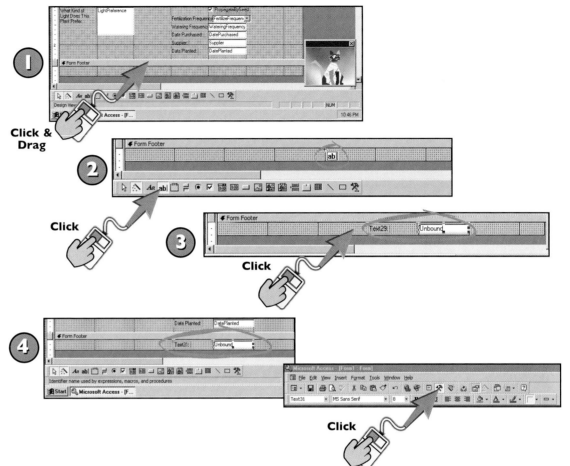

Click & Drag

Click

Click

Click

Click

1. Drag the **Form Footer** bar up so that you can view everything in a single screen.

2. Click the Text Box button on the toolbox and bring it up to the form footer area.

3. Click once and Access will place an unbound text box on the form footer.

4. Select the text box field—it says **Unbound** inside it—and then click the Properties button on the toolbar. The property sheet for the text box displays.

Next Step

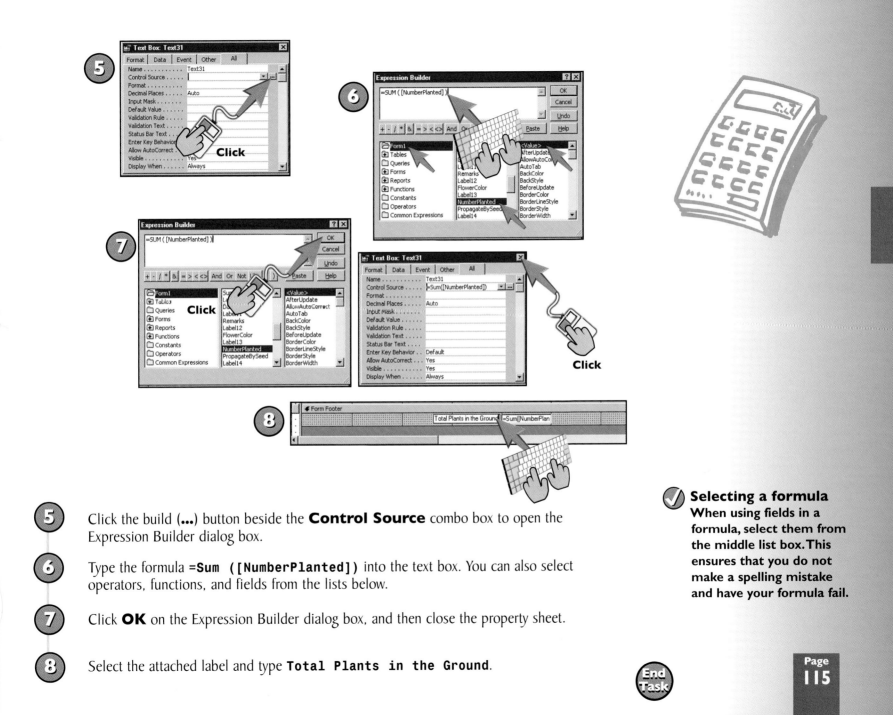

Text Box: Text31
Format | Data | Event | Other | All
Name Text31
Control Source . . . . .
Format . . . .
Decimal Places . . . . . Auto
Input Mask . . . .
Default Value . . . . . .
Validation Rule . . . . .
Validation Text . . . . .
Status Bar Text . . . .
Enter Key Behavior . .
Allow AutoCorrect . .
Visible . . . . Yes
Display When . . . . . . Always

Click

Expression Builder
=SUM ([NumberPlanted])
OK
Cancel
Undo
Help
+ - / * & = > < <> And Or
Paste
Form1
Tables
Queries
Forms
Reports
Functions
Constants
Operators
Common Expressions

Remarks
Label12
FlowerColor
Label13
NumberPlanted
PropagateBySeed
Label14

<Value>
AfterUpdate
AllowAutoColor
AutoTab
BackColor
BackStyle
BeforeUpdate
BorderColor
BorderLineStyle
BorderStyle
BorderWidth

Expression Builder
=SUM ([NumberPlanted])
OK
Cancel
Undo
Help
+ - / * & = > < <> And Or Not
Paste

Click

Form1
Tables
Queries
Forms
Reports
Functions
Constants
Operators
Common Expressions

Remarks
Label12
FlowerColor
Label13
NumberPlanted
PropagateBySeed
Label14

<Value>
AfterUpdate
AllowAutoCorrect
AutoTab
BackColor
BackStyle
BeforeUpdate
BorderColor
BorderLineStyle
BorderStyle
BorderWidth

Text Box: Text31
Format | Data | Event | Other | All
Name Text31
Control Source . . . . . =Sum([NumberPlanted])
Format . . . .
Decimal Places . . . . . Auto
Input Mask . . . .
Default Value . . . . . .
Validation Rule . . . . .
Validation Text . . . . .
Status Bar Text . . . .
Enter Key Behavior . . Default
Allow AutoCorrect . . . Yes
Visible . . . . Yes
Display When . . . . . . Always

Click

Form Footer
Total Plants in the Ground | =Sum([NumberPlan

(5) Click the build (**...**) button beside the **Control Source** combo box to open the Expression Builder dialog box.

(6) Type the formula **=Sum ([NumberPlanted])** into the text box. You can also select operators, functions, and fields from the lists below.

(7) Click **OK** on the Expression Builder dialog box, and then close the property sheet.

(8) Select the attached label and type **Total Plants in the Ground**.

✓ **Selecting a formula**
When using fields in a formula, select them from the middle list box. This ensures that you do not make a spelling mistake and have your formula fail.

End Task

Task 14: Adding Pop-Up Tip Text to Fields

In addition to the other forms of help you have learned to use, Access enables you to create your own pop-up tips that display when a user pauses the mouse pointer on a field in the form. These tips act just like the ToolTips you see when you place the mouse on a tool on the toolbar.

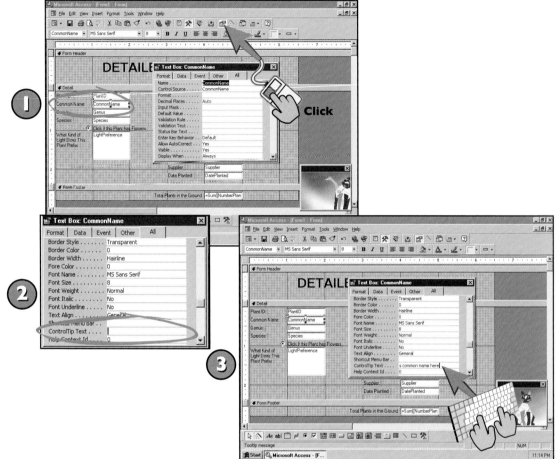

✓ **If text does not fit**
It's OK if the text scrolls out of view. You can enter a maximum of 256 characters for a tip.

1 Select the **CommonName** field and then click the Properties button on the toolbar.

2 On the properties sheet move down the list until you come to the **ControlTip Text** property.

3 Type **Type the Plant's common name here**.

Next Step

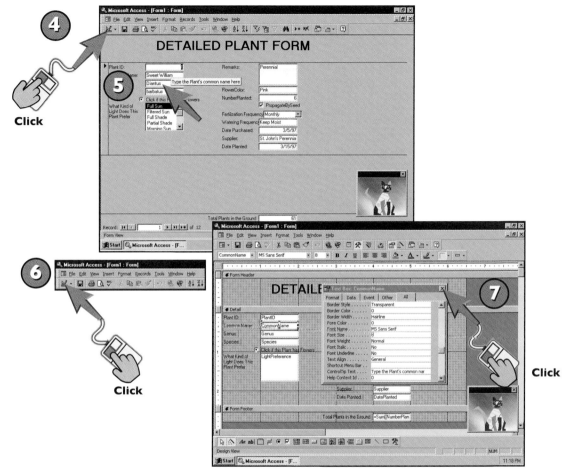

4 Click the View button on the toolbar and the form will be displayed in Form view.

5 Place the mouse pointer on the **CommonName** field and see the tip displayed. This is a good method of seeing what your form currently looks like.

6 Click the View button again to return to form design view.

7 Close the property sheet by clicking the Close (X) button.

Task 15: Saving Your New Form

After you have completed your form, you must save it or you will lose all your work. Access doesn't automatically save a form created in Design view as it did the form created with the wizard. When you save the form, it is placed on the Forms list and will be available for later use.

Start Here

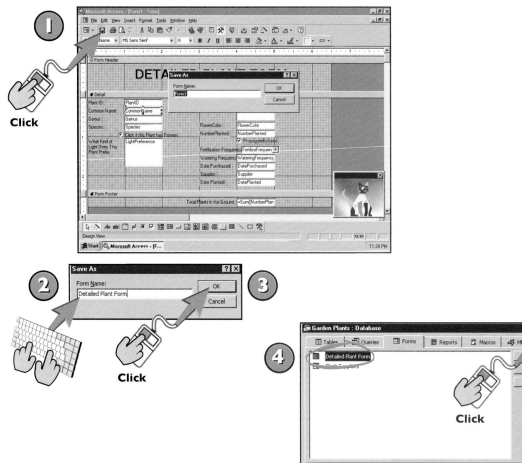

Click

Click

Click

✓ **Save shortcuts**
You can also select **File, Save** from the menu, or press the **Ctrl+S** keyboard shortcut to do the same thing.

1 Click the Save button on the toolbar and the Save As dialog box displays.

2 Type **Detailed Plant Form** into the **Form Name** text box. This is the name that will be displayed on the Forms list in the Database window.

3 Click **OK**.

4 Click the Close (X) button on the form window. You will now see your form in the Forms list.

End Task

Task 16: Opening a Form

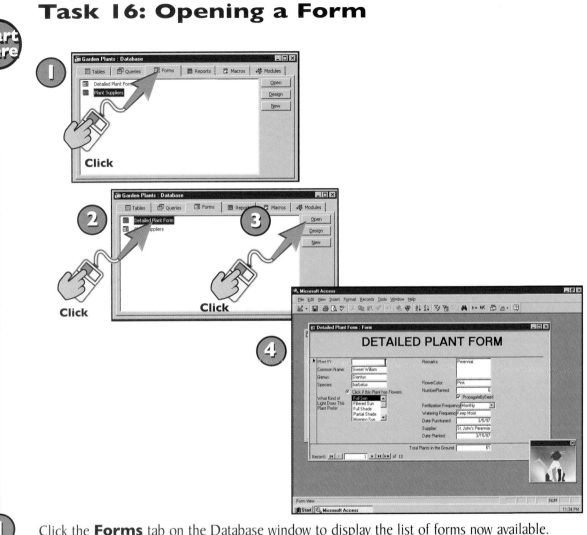

Click

Click **Click**

Just like a table on which a form is based, you must open the form before you can do any work with it. After you open the form, you can enter or edit information in the table. Remember that the form is simply another way to view the information contained in the table.

---

① Click the **Forms** tab on the Database window to display the list of forms now available.

② Click the form that you want to open, in this case **Detailed Plant Form**.

③ Click **Open**.

④ The selected form is displayed. If it is not sized correctly, maximize the display or resize the window so that you can see as much of the form as needed.

Task 17: Entering and Editing Information with a Form

For most users the form is the most familiar method of entering or editing information. Everyone is comfortable using a form, and creating a form that is similar to a paper form you now use will eliminate many mistakes.

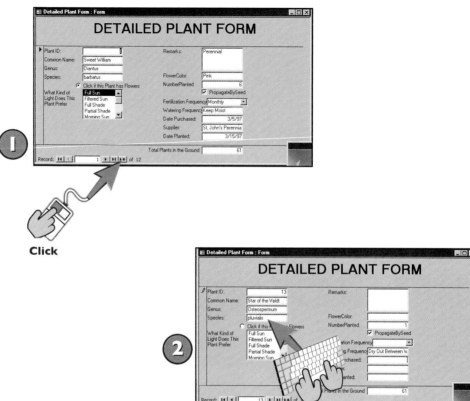

Click

 The field tab order
If you delete a field and then replace it on the form, the tab index changes. This is why the cursor doesn't move smoothly from field to field.

1 Before you can enter new information into a table, you must get to a blank record. Click the New Record button.

2 Press Tab to move to the **Common Name** field and type **Star of the Veldt**. Type **Osteospermum** in the **Genus** field and **pluvialis** in the **Species** field, pressing Tab after each.

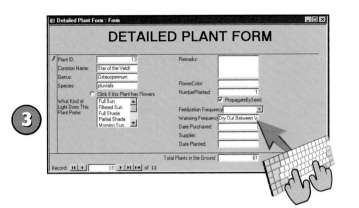

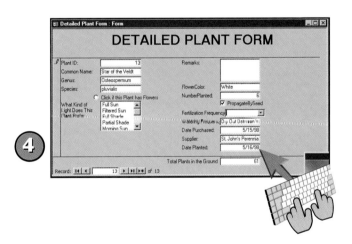

3 Press Tab again. The cursor now jumps to the **Watering Frequency** field. Type **Dry Out Between Watering**, and press Tab again.

4 Type **5/15/98** in the **Date Purchased** field and press Tab. Type **St. John's Perennials** in **Supplier** and **5/16/98** in **Date Planted**. Press Tab twice and type **White** in **FlowerColor** and **6** in **NumberPlanted**, and press Tab twice.

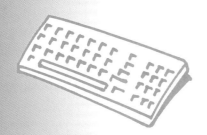

Entering and Editing Information with a Form Continued

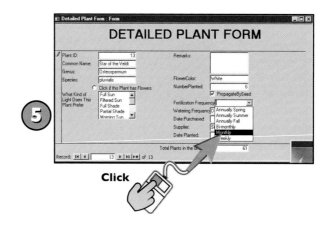

⑤ Click

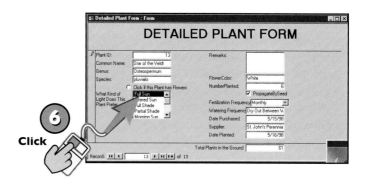

⑥ Click

⑤ The cursor should be in the **Fertilization Frequency** field. Click the arrow button on the combo box and select **Monthly** from the list. Press Tab.

⑥ In the **What Kind of Light Does This Plant Prefer** list box select the option **Full Sun** and press Tab.

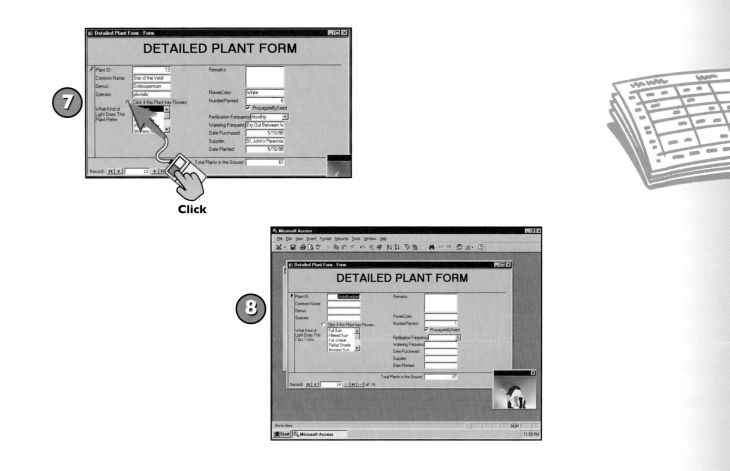

Click

---

7 The cursor is now at the option button. Click once to indicate this plant does produce flowers.

8 Press Tab once more. A new blank record is displayed. You can enter a new record, and the one you just completed is automatically saved in the table.

Task 18: Changing the Field Order

The order in which the cursor moves from field to field on the form is called the tab index. In order for a form to work well for you, the cursor should move from one field to the next, and not bounce around the screen.

The tab index is based on the order in which you placed a field on the form. You added all the fields once, but you also deleted several and then replaced them with other controls. This removed them from the tab index order and then added them back at the end. Changing the tab index is simple.

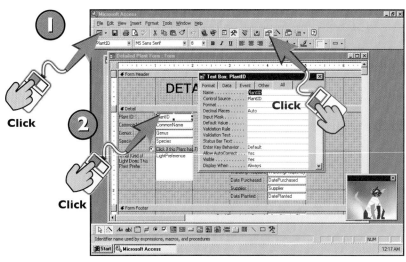

Click

Click

Click

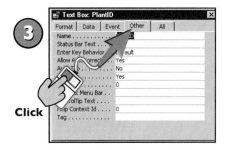

Click

① Click the View button to switch the form to Design view.

② Select the **PlantID** field on your form and click the Properties button.

③ Click the **Other** tab on the property sheet. This limits the display to only a few properties, including Tab Index and Tab Stop.

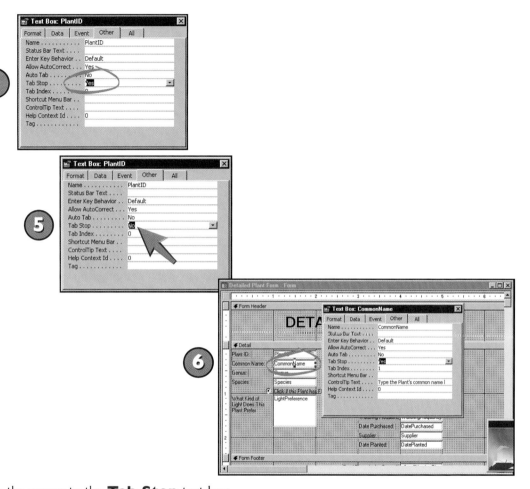

 4 Move the cursor to the **Tab Stop** text box.

5 Change this option from **Yes** to **No**. The Tab Stop property determines whether the cursor stops at the field or passes it. When set to **No**, the field is passed when the Tab key is pressed.

6 Select **CommonName** on the form to display its property sheet. The **Tab Stop** is set to **Yes**, and the **Tab Index** is set to the number **1**; these don't need changing.

 Setting tab stops
When a tab stop is set to **No**, you don't need to worry about the Tab Index setting. The first field placed on a form is always Tab Index 0.

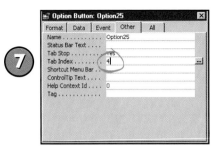

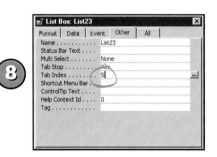

✓ No duplicate tab index numbers

Access doesn't allow you create duplicate tab index numbers. For example, if you change tab index 13 to 3, then the field that was tab index 3 would become 4, and so on back to 9, which would now be 10.

⑦ Continue to select each field in the order that you want them selected when Tab is pressed. Check the Tab Index number for each field ensuring that it is one greater than the previous. Change the option button **Plant Flowers** from **14** to **4**.

⑧ Change the **LightPreference** tab index from **14** to **5**.

Next Step

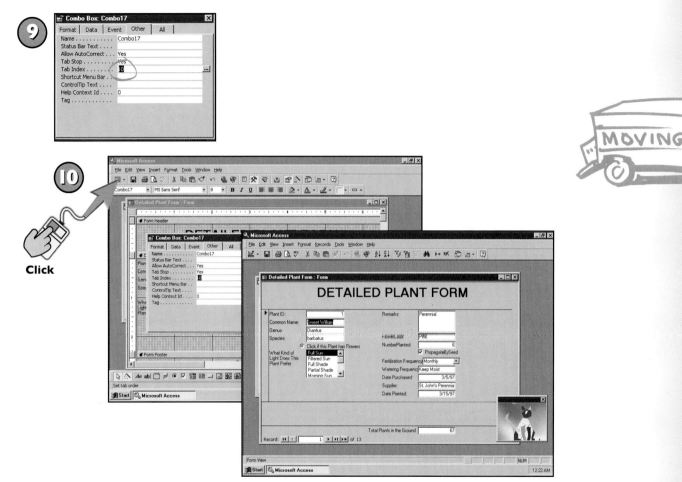

9   Change the tab index properties: Remarks, **6**; FlowerColor, **7**; NumberPlanted, **8**; PropagateBySeed, **9**; FertilizeFrequency, **10**. Access will adjust the remaining fields.

10   Click the View button and tab through a record to see if everything works as you expect.

✓ **Move the property sheet**

If the property sheet is in the way, drag it from one side of the screen to the other so that it doesn't cover a field you need to select.

PART 5

Getting Information from the Database

The capability to ask questions about the information in your database is one of the most powerful features in Access. A question is built in the form of an example and is called a *query*. Unlike a simple file in which you can look up one record at a time, Access can respond to a query by finding and displaying all records that meet certain *criteria*. Criteria are the set of restrictions that you place on what information is to be found—the *result set*.

You can use several types of queries, each of which produces a different result. The following are most commonly used:

Select query: Enables you to select and display a group of records. This will be a subset of the entire table; for example, all customers who live in the state of California.

Crosstab query: Use this query when you are sifting through a great deal of data looking for trends, or to generate summaries. You can also use this to create graphs about the data.

Action query: Use this query to add or update data in your table. For example, you can increase the selling price of all items now priced at $5 or more by 10 percent.

Like a table, a query can be used as the basis of a report or form. Queries can be used to display information from several tables in a single form or report. When you first start creating your own queries, write them down. This will help you focus on the information you are looking for.

Tasks

Task 1: Opening Query Design View

The most common query that you will use is the select query. You can use it to choose records that meet the criteria you specify, and then display the result set in a datasheet (a table-like view).

In this example, you will create a query for the statement "Display all records for plants that have white flowers, including only the Common Name, Genus, Species, and Number Planted."

Start Here

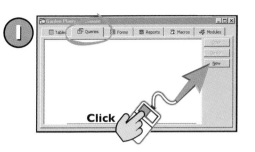
Click

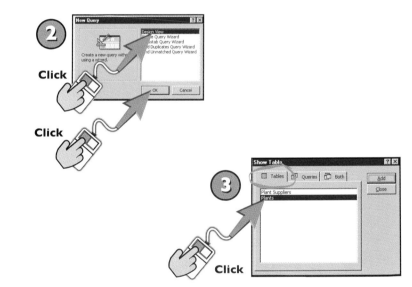
Click
Click
Click

(1) Select the **Queries** tab on the Database window, and then click the **New** button. Access displays the New Query dialog box.

(2) Select the **Design View** option, and then click **OK**.

(3) Select the **Tables** tab on the Show Tables dialog box and then select **Plants** from the list.

Next Step

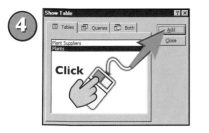

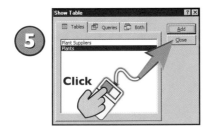

The asterisk and the Query Design grid
Selecting the asterisk will
[...]
table. It will automatically include any field added to the table later, or remove any field deleted from the table.

(4) Click **Add** to place it into the Query Design view window.

(5) Click the **Close** button because this query is based on just this one table.

(6) From the **Plants** field list box double-click the field **CommonName**. Access immediately places the field on the query grid.

Opening Query Design View Continued

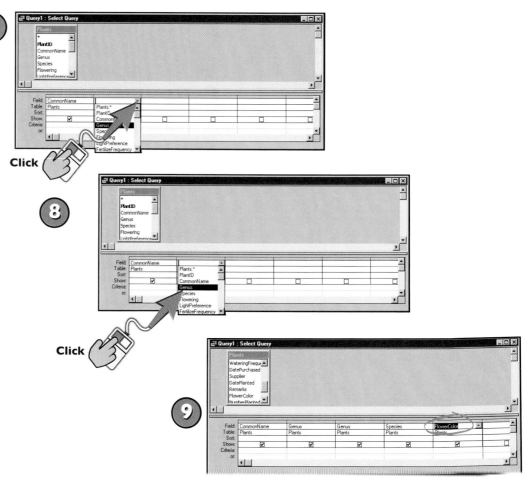

Click

Click

Scroll to view more fields

If you can't see a field on the query grid, use the horizontal scrollbar to see whether it is simply too far to the right to be seen. You can resize a column by dragging the right edge of any column selector button.

 Click the mouse inside the **Field** row of the second column of the grid and click the arrow button

Select **Genus** as the second field for this query and **Species** and **NumberPlanted** as the third and fourth columns.

Place **FlowerColor** as the last field in the query grid.

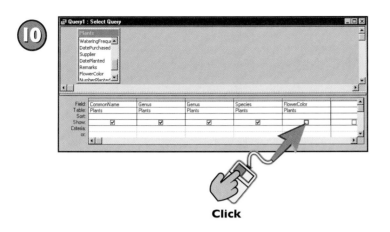

Click

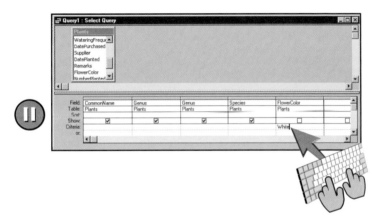

10 Click the check box in the **Show** row of **FlowerColor**, removing the check mark to indicate that this field won't display in the result set. You can use a field as a criterion or for sorting but not show it.

11 Click in the **Criteria** row of the **FlowerColor** column and type **White**. This is the actual criterion that a record must meet before it will be included in the result set.

Task 2: Running and Saving a Query

After you have set up a query in the Query Design view grid, you can run the query or view the result set. For a select query, both of these terms mean the same thing. For any type of action query, *viewing* simply shows you the records to which the specified action will apply: these records will be updated, deleted, and so on. *Running* the query will actually apply the action to the selected records.

After you have created a query and it does what you expect of it, you can save it for later use. I highly recommend saving a query because clicking on the query to run it again is much easier than trying to re-create a complex query.

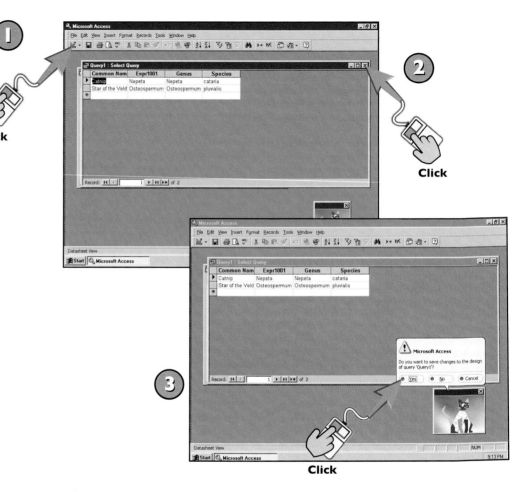

Click

Click

Click

Click

① Click the **View** button on the toolbar to see the result set for this query.

② Click the Close (X) button after you have viewed the results.

③ The Office Assistant displays a balloon asking if you want to save this query; click the **Yes** button.

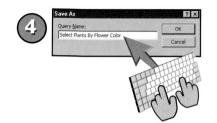

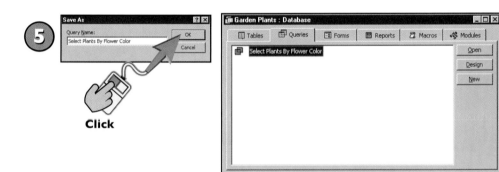

Click

In the Save As dialog box type **Select Plants By Flower Color** in the text box.

Click **OK**. The new query is added to the **Queries** list in the Database window. You can reuse this query to choose plants with a color other than white by changing the color criteria from White to another color.

✔ **Reworking the query**
If the query doesn't
perform as expected,

~~button again to return to~~
the Design View window.
Make any necessary
adjustments and then view
the new result set.

End
Task

Task 3: Using the Crosstab Query

Although a table is an efficient method of storing information, it is rarely the best format for analyzing data. Access has a special query, called a *crosstab query*, designed specifically to help you summarize data. It can show values by comparing the data from one field with the data in another.

In this task you will create a crosstab query to answer the query statement, "How many plants of each color have I planted?" This statement compares the number of plants you have by their color.

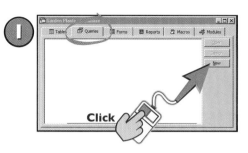

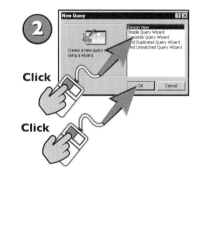

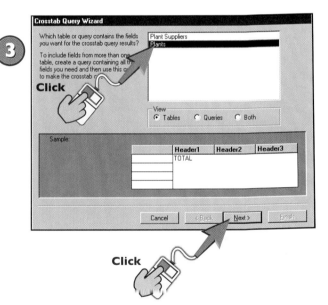

Click the **Queries** tab, and then click the **New** button.

Select **Crosstab Query Wizard** from the New Query dialog box, and then click **OK**.

The first Crosstab Query Wizard dialog box appears. Select the **Plants** table from the list and then click the **Next>** button.

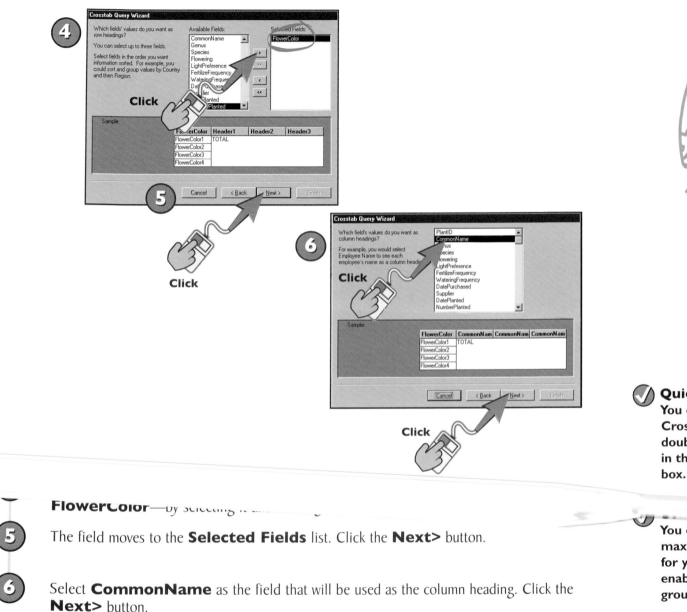

Click

Click

Click

Quick open
You can quickly open the
Crosstab Query Wizard by
double-clicking the option
in the New Query dialog
box.

FlowerColor—by selecting it and

⑤ The field moves to the **Selected Fields** list. Click the **Next>** button.

⑥ Select **CommonName** as the field that will be used as the column heading. Click the
Next> button.

You can choose a
maximum of three fields
for your row headers,
enabling you to sort and
group fields.

Using the Crosstab Query Continued

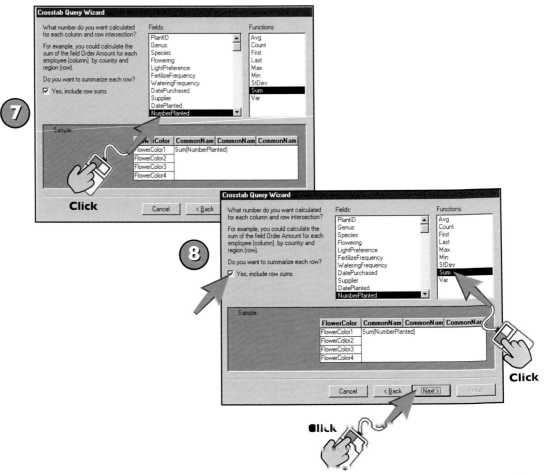

7 Choose the field to be used to compare the previously selected fields to each other. Here you're comparing numbers of plants by color and name, so select the **NumberPlanted** field.

8 Choose the type of summary calculation you want; select the **Sum** function. Be sure the box **Yes, include row sums** is selected, and then click **Next>**.

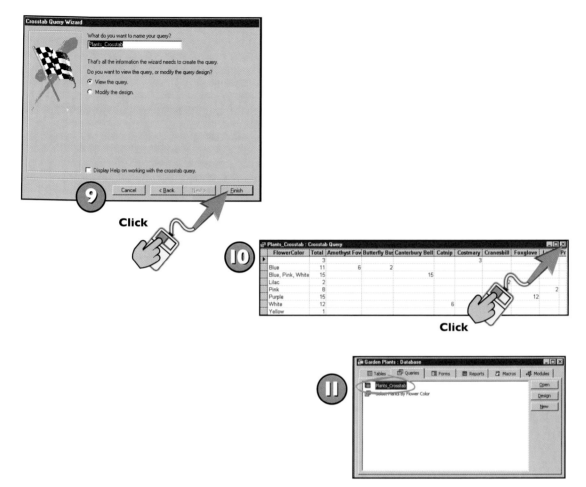

Click

Click

End
Task

Enter a title for the query—the default title is fine. Click the **Finish** button.

Click the Close (X) button.

Your **Queries** list appears. A query created with a wizard is automatically saved.

✓ **The result set**
The result set is displayed in a datasheet view. Each of the various flower colors is listed in the left column, while the common name is shown as column titles. A summary column, giving you the total number of plants in each color, is displayed as the second

will see that **Costmary** has no color listed; either you didn't enter a color or the plant doesn't have a flower.

Task 4: Selecting Records with Wildcards

Many times, when you want to search for information you might not know exactly how something is spelled or you might want to find all records that meet a partial criterion. For example, you might want to find all customers whose names begin with the letter **B**. Access gives you a set of *wildcard* characters that you can use in the place of other letters.

The most common wildcard characters are the asterisk (*) and the question mark (?). An asterisk represents any number of any characters, and the question mark represents any single character.

 I lick the **Queries** tab, and then click the **New** button.

Select **Design View** from the list box, and then click **OK**.

Select **Plants** from the Show Table dialog box, and click the **Add** button.

Click the **Close** button.

Next Step

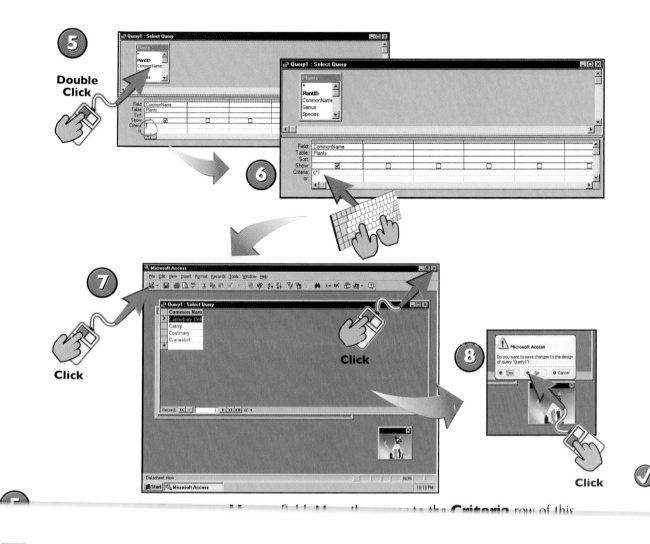

Page
141

A blank result set
If you see a result set with no records, this means that ʌ... .... ʌ........ ..... again. If it's correct, you might want to manually check the table for such records.

6 Type **c*** to tell Access to search for all plants with a common name beginning with the letter C. Press an arrow key or click the mouse in another cell. Access changes the criteria to **Like "c*"**.

7 Click the View button on the toolbar to see the result set. Click the Close (X) button.

8 When the Office Assistant prompts you to save the new query, select the **No** button.

Task 5: Selecting Records with an OR Criteria

Often, you will want to find records that meet either one criterion or another. In this task you want to find all plants that have either blue or white flowers. A query that says "Select this or select that" uses an **OR** operator and tells Access to select any record that meets at least one of the criterion; it doesn't have to meet both.

OR criteria can be set up across multiple fields. For example, a query that asks "Select customers from the state of **NY** or from the city of Los Angeles" uses a multiple-field **OR** criteria.

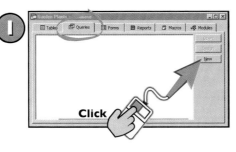

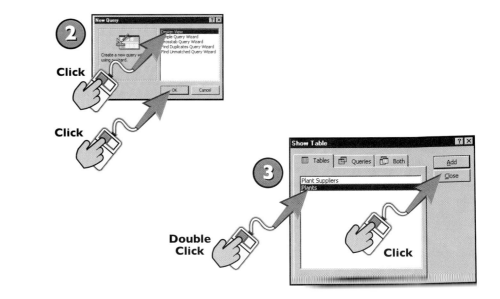

 Open the **Queries** list and click the **New** button.

 Select **Design View** from the list and click **OK**.

(3) Double-click the **Plants** table for this query, and then **Close** the Show Tables dialog box.

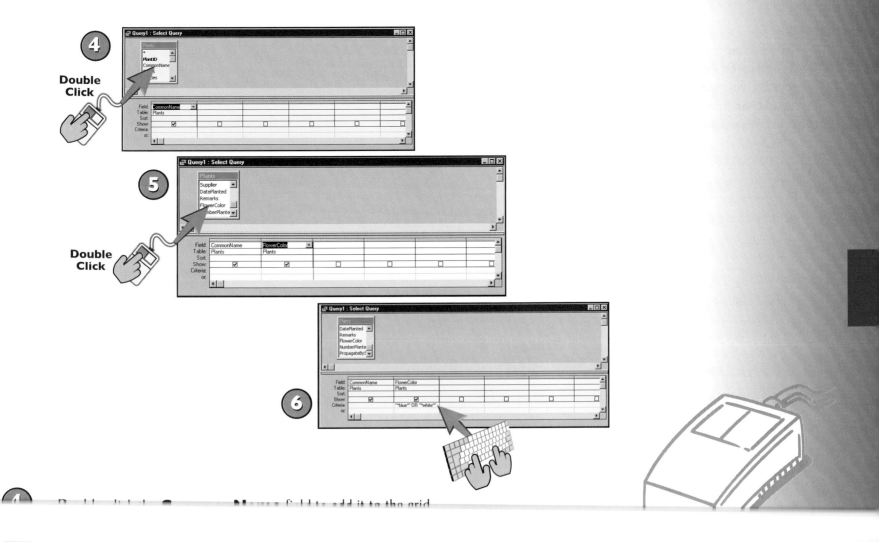

Double-click the **CommonName** field to add it to the grid.

5 Double-click the **FlowerColor** field to add it to the grid.

6 In the **Criteria** row of the **FlowerColor** column type `"*blue*" OR "*white*"` and then press the up arrow key.

Next Step

Selecting Records with an OR Criteria Continued

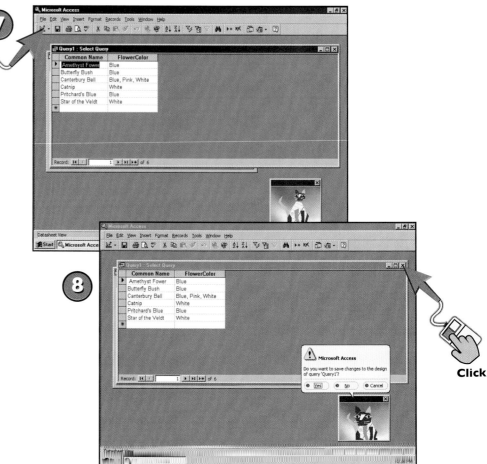

Click

Click

Why wildcards?
The asterisk wildcard ensures that plants with multiple flower colors will also be included.

One line or two?
An OR criteria can be broken into two parts and placed in separate rows. Notice that the row below the **Criteria** row is labeled **or**. You could type the first criteria "*blue*" in the **Criteria** row, and then the second "*white*" into the second row, directly beneath the first.

⑦ Click the View button to see the result set.

⑧ When you have viewed the result set, click the Close (X) button.

Next Step

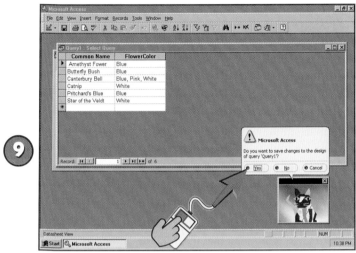

Click

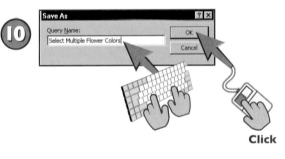

Click

Type **Select Multiple Flower Colors** in the Save As dialog box, and then click **OK**.

There will be times when you must find records that meet multiple criteria—for example, all customers who live in New York and who purchased blue widgets this year.

For a customer to be included in the result set of this query, he must meet all criteria: living in New York, *and* having purchased blue widgets, *and* having made the purchase this year. This is an example of a query using an **AND** operator. In this task, you will use an **AND** operator to find all plants with blue flowers **AND** that require full

AND and criteria rows
You must enter the criteria in the same row for them to be considered an AND operator. Criteria entered in separate rows are considered to be OR criteria.

Task 6: Selecting Records with More than One Criterion

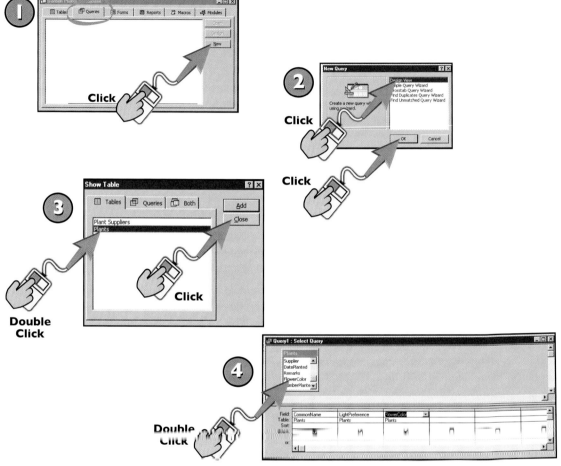

1 Open the **Queries** list and click the **New** button.

2 Select **Design View** from the list and click **OK**.

3 Double-click the **Plants** table for this query, and then **Close** the Show Tables dialog box.

4 Double-click **CommonName**, **LightPreference**, and **FlowerColor** from the Plants list box.

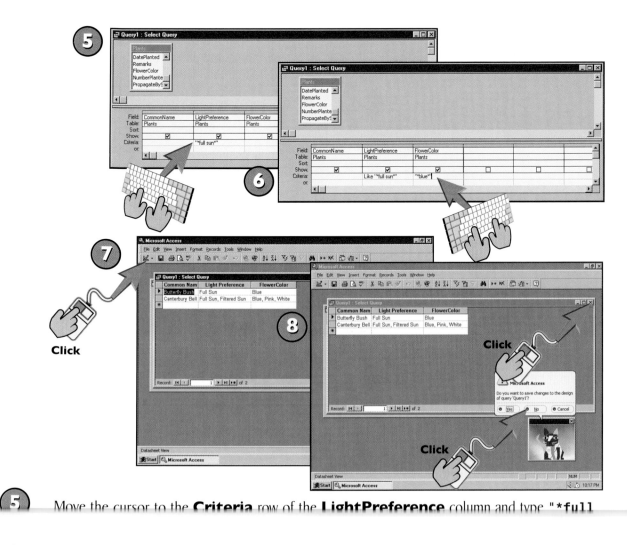

Click

Click

Click

⑤ Move the cursor to the **Criteria** row of the **LightPreference** column and type "*full

⑥ Move the cursor to the **Criteria** row for the **FlowerColor** column and type "*blue*",
and then click in another cell. Access adds the comparative operator **Like** to both criteria.

⑦ Click the View button to see the result set. Two records match the criteria. Notice the second
record would have been excluded without the wildcard in the color criteria.

⑧ Click the Close (X) button, and don't save the query when prompted by the Office
Assistant.

 **Extra records**
If your result set includes

check the query grid again.
Be sure you didn't add the
criteria on different rows
and accidentally create an
OR query instead.

End
Task

Page
147

Task 7: Using Arithmetic Operators

The most commonly used arithmetic operators include equal (=), plus (+), less than (<), greater than (>), less than or equal to (<=), and greater than or equal to (>=). These operators can be used with both text and numeric data. In contrast, these operators are used only with numeric information: minus (-), multiply (*), and divide (/).

In this task, you can use an arithmetic operator in a query to display records and create a query that displays all plants with blue flowers that you planted on or after January 1, 1997.

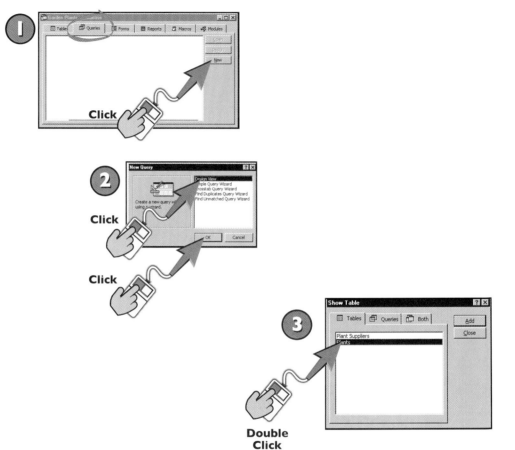

 Open the **Queries** list and click the **New** button.

Select **Design View** from the list and click **OK**.

Double-click the **Plants** table for this query.

Click

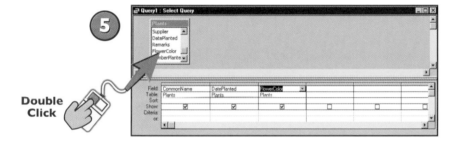

Double Click

4 **Close** the Show Table dialog box.

... the Plants ... **CommonName**, **DatePlanted**, and **FlowerColor**, placing each onto the query grid.

An AND operator ...

meet both criteria, the query uses an **AND** operator. Be sure you enter both criteria on the same row.

Using Arithmetic Operators Continued

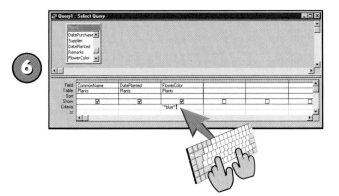

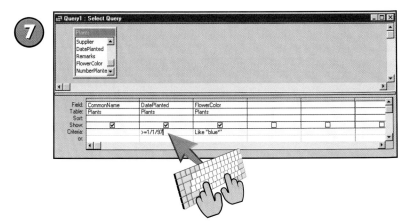

 Move the cursor to the **Criteria** row in the **FlowerColor** column and type **"*blue*"** as the entry.

 Move the cursor to the **Criteria** row in the **DatePlanted** column and type **>=1/1/97**. Access changes this entry to read **>=#1/1/97#**. In a query, the two **#** symbols indicate that the numbers between them are a date value.

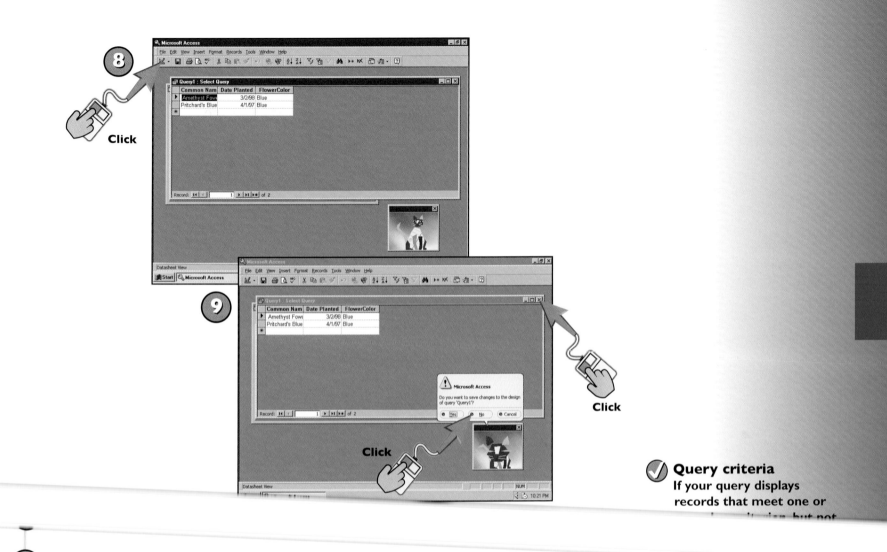

Click the Close (X) button, and don't save the query when prompted by the Office Assistant.

✅ **Query criteria**
If your query displays records that meet one or ~~...~~ *criteria, but not*

the criteria on separate lines. Make sure that the criteria statements are on the same line to create an **AND** query.

Page
151

Task 8: Adding a New Field

You can use a query to display fields that are not actually part of the underlying table. This is often done when you plan to use the query as the basis for a form or report. For example, in a report you might want to combine fields such as Last Name and First Name so that they will print together without a large space between them.

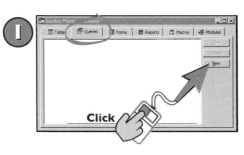

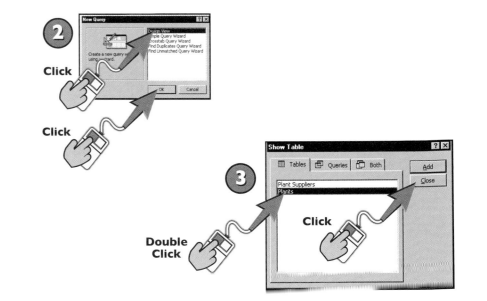

 On the **Queries** tab, click the **New** button.

 Select **Design View**, and then click **OK**.

 Double-click **Plants**, and then click the **Close** button.

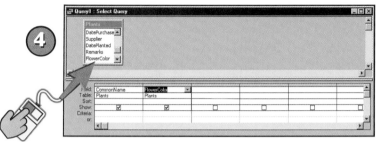

**Double
Click**

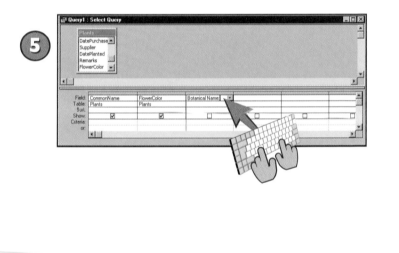

the query grid.

Move the cursor to the blank column beside **FlowerColor** on the grid, in the **Field** row, and type **Botanical Name:**—be sure to end with the (:) colon.

End
Task

Task 9: Calculating a Value with a Query

A calculated field in a query can manipulate values from two numeric fields or from text fields. For example, you can calculate two numeric values like this: **Extended Price: [Quantity] * [SellPrice]**. This example creates a new field named **Extended Price** populated with the value from multiplying the value in the Quantity field by the value in the SellPrice field.

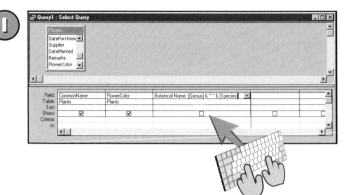

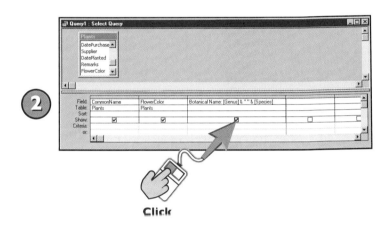

Click

In the newly created field **Botanical Name:** create the calculation by typing `[Genus]&" "&[Species]`.

Click in the **Show** check box so that the new field will be displayed in the result set.

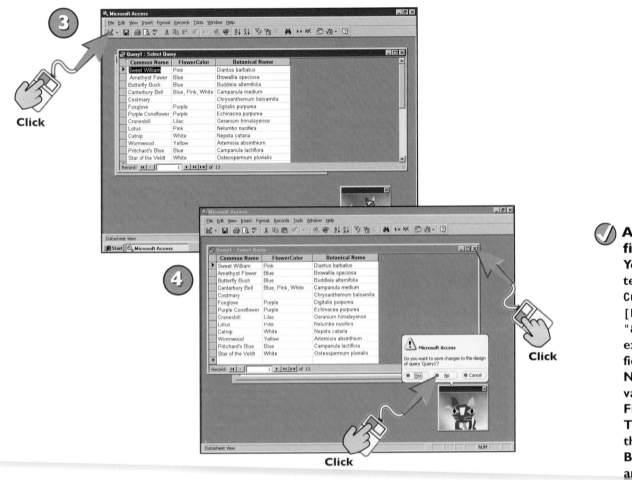

3

Click

Click

4

Click

Click the Close (X) button, and then the **No** button when prompted to save the new query.

✔ Additional calculated field examples

You can also combine two text fields like this: `Customer Name: [FirstName]&" "&[LastName].` This example creates a new field called **Customer Name**. It is filled with the values from the fields FirstName and LastName. The ampersand (&) adds the fields together. Between the two ampersands is a space

the single space in the customer's name.

Calculated fields like these two examples are not normally saved in a table.

Task 10: Deleting Records with a Query

You can create an action query that will delete unwanted records. You can delete records one by one, but if you must remove many records and they can be ferreted out using criteria, you can use a **Delete query**. In order for this to be worth the time and effort, the records must be selectable as a group. For example, you could create a query that would delete all customer records for those customers who have not purchased products in the last three years. This is a selectable group of records.

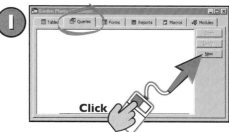

Click

 Click

Click

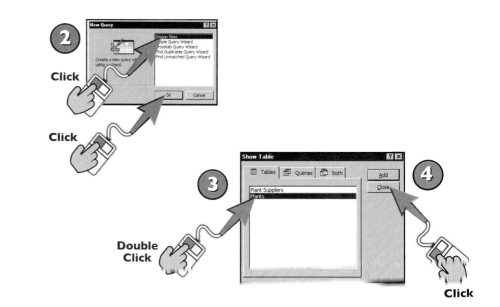

Double
Click

Click

On the **Queries** tab, click the **New** button.

Select **Design View**, and then click **OK**.

Double-click **Plants**.

Click the **Close** button.

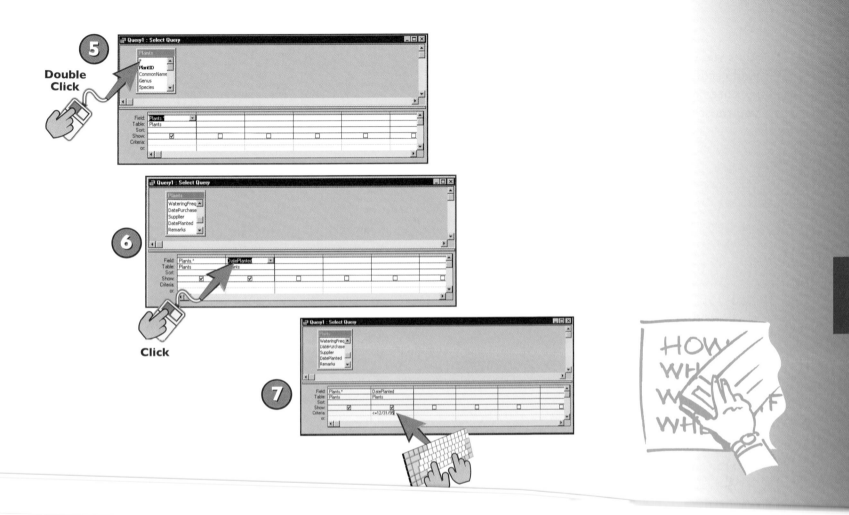

fields contained in the table.

6 Click the **DatePlanted** field. This will be the field that you use for a criteria to select records.

7 In the **Criteria** row of the **DatePlanted** column type **<=12/31/95**. This selects all records that were planted on or before December 31, 1995.

Deleting Records with a Query Continued

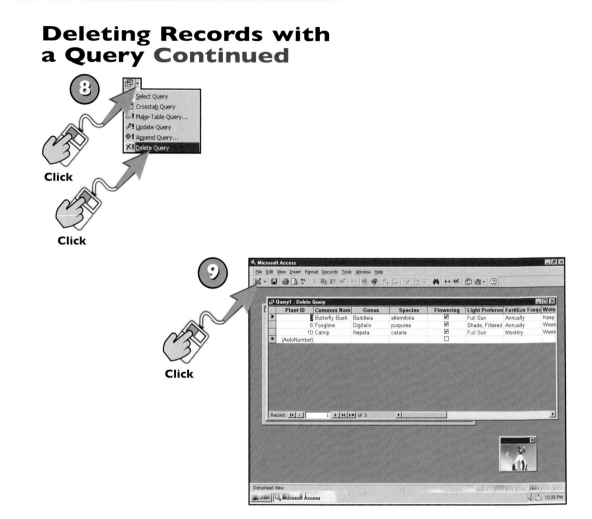

Click

Click

Click

8️⃣ Click the down-arrow part of the Query Type button on the toolbar, and select **Delete Query** from the list. This is an action query.

9️⃣ Click the View button to see that three records are selected by the query.

Next Step

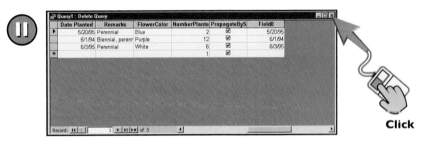

Click

10 Scroll to the **DatePlanted** column to verify that these records meet the criteria. The records will be deleted if you click the Run button on the Query Design view toolbar.

11 Click the Close (X) button, and don't save the query when prompted by the Office Assistant.

Task 11: Creating a Query That Prompts for a Criteria Variable

Sometimes you will create a query for a single purpose, but later decide that you want to use it again with slightly different criteria. For example, earlier you created the **"Select Plants By Flower Color"** query that displayed all plants with white flowers. If you want to use this query to find plants with blue flowers, you could edit the query and change the criterion from white to blue. Alternatively, you can change the criteria to always prompt you for the color that you want to find—this is called a *parameter* query.

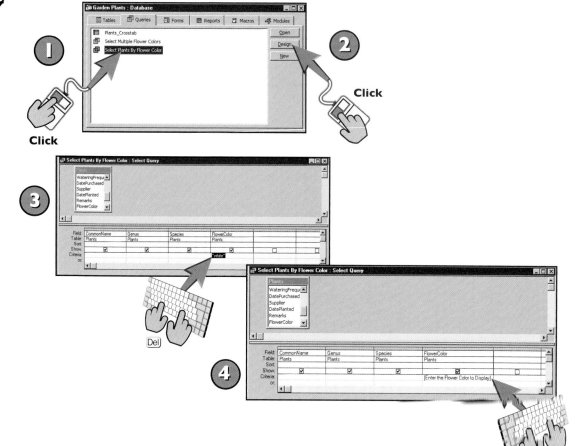

Click

Click

 In the Queries window, click the **Select Plants By Flower Color** query.

 Click the **Design** button.

 Select the criteria **"white"** and press the Delete key.

 Type **[Enter the Flower Color to Display]**. Be sure the check box in this column is checked.

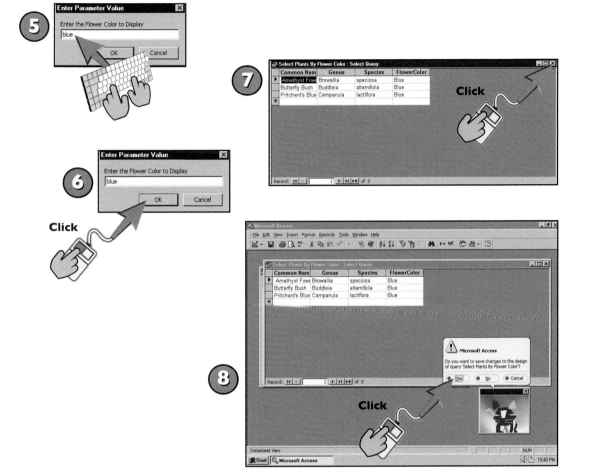

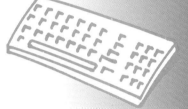

5. Click the View button, and then type **blue** in the Parameter dialog box that is displayed.

6. Click **OK** to view the result set.

7. Click the Close (X) button.

8. Click **Yes** when prompted to save the changes to the query.

PART

6

Creating and Using Reports

Although you can print copies of tables, forms, and query datasheets, you have much greater control over the format when it is printed as a report. Many of the techniques you learned for building a form can be used to create a report. With a report, you will also learn to group records and create summary information such as totals, subtotals, and percentages. Summary data can be shown for groups of records and for the report as a whole.

Reports are often based on queries rather than on tables. This lets you select only the included records instead of automatically reporting on all records. When you use a query as the basis of the report, the query is run when you access the report, and then the report is displayed or printed.

You can create reports for mailing labels, invoices, product tags, address and phone lists, sales and purchase analyses, sales contacts, and any other information that you store in a table.

Tasks

Task 1: Building a Report with a Wizard

You have learned to use tables to store information, you have created forms to work with the data, and you have learned to use queries to search for specific information. Now suddenly your boss wants a report on her desk by quitting time today. What should you do?

By using the Report Wizard, you can quickly create a report that has a polished, professional appearance. You have a choice of several styles for the layout and how records will be grouped.

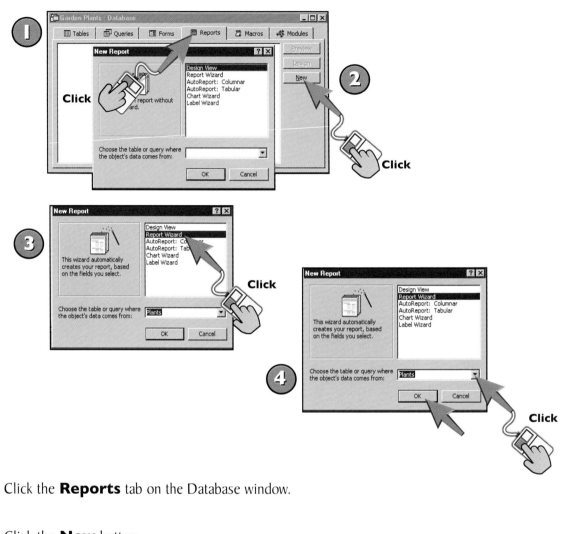

(1) Click the **Reports** tab on the Database window.

(2) Click the **New** button.

(3) From the New Report dialog box select **Report Wizard** from the list box.

(4) Select **Plants** from the combo box below the list, and then click **OK**.

Next Step

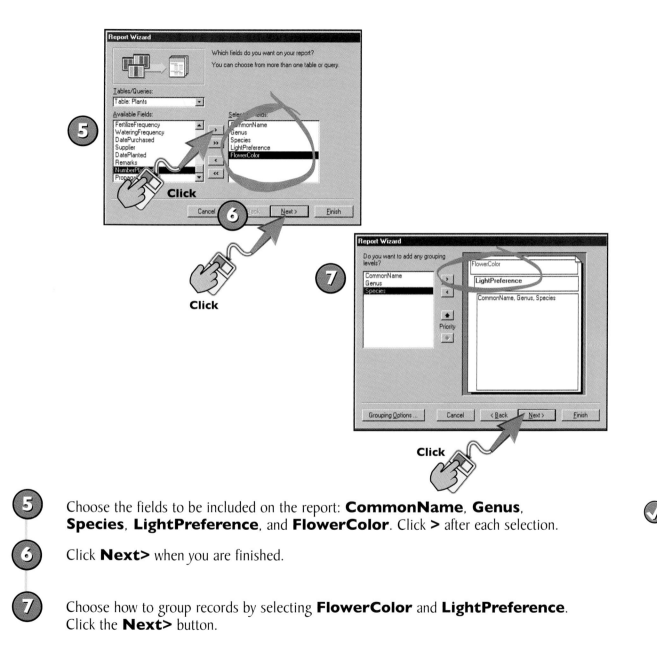

5 Choose the fields to be included on the report: **CommonName**, **Genus**, **Species**, **LightPreference**, and **FlowerColor**. Click **>** after each selection.

6 Click **Next>** when you are finished.

7 Choose how to group records by selecting **FlowerColor** and **LightPreference**. Click the **Next>** button.

✓ Report Details
These choices tell Access to group records first by flower color, and then subdivide the first group by the plant's light preference.

Building a Report with a Wizard Continued

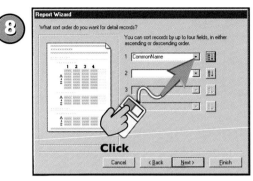

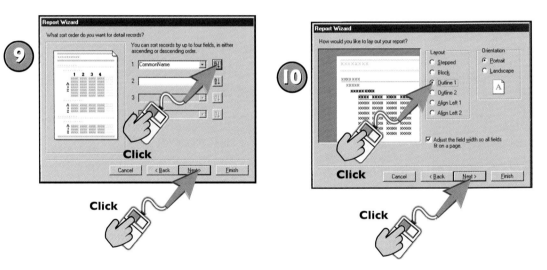

 Landscape or portrait
If you have more than eight detail fields selected, you might want to use landscape mode for printing. This will print the report across the page instead of down the page.

8 Select **CommonName** as the field for sorting the detail records in the first combo box.

9 Select ascending or descending sort order from the button beside the combo box. Click the **Next>** button.

10 Select **Outline 1** for this report. You can view a sample of each report layout by clicking each in turn. Click **Next>**.

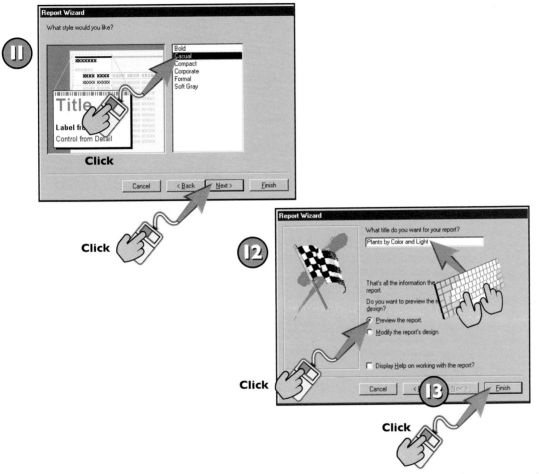

11 Select a style and font for the report titles. You have six options; click through them to see what each looks like. Click the **Casual** option from the list and then click the **Next>** button.

12 Type **Plants by Color and Light** in the text box as the title for the report, and then click the **Preview the report** option button.

13 Click the **Finish** button to complete the report.

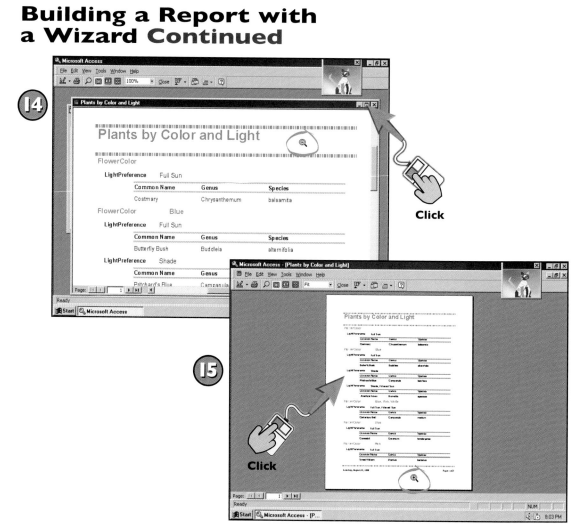

Building a Report with a Wizard Continued

Click

Click

14 Click the Maximize button so that you can see more of the report. Notice the mouse pointer changes to a magnifying glass with a minus sign in the lens.

15 Click the mouse anywhere on the report and see the report shrink so that you can easily see a page layout. The mouse changes to show a plus sign in the lens.

Next Step

Click the arrow button on the **Zoom** combo box and select **75%** from the list. The report changes size to 75% of actual size.

Close the report by clicking the **Close** button on the toolbar. The report is displayed in the Reports window.

Task 2: Opening the Report Design View

Like most other Access objects, you can create a new report or edit an existing one in the Report Design view window. The Report Design view window is similar to the Form Design view window. The grid and many of the tools are the same. Selecting an object, table, or query, and then opening the Report Design view window is the first step.

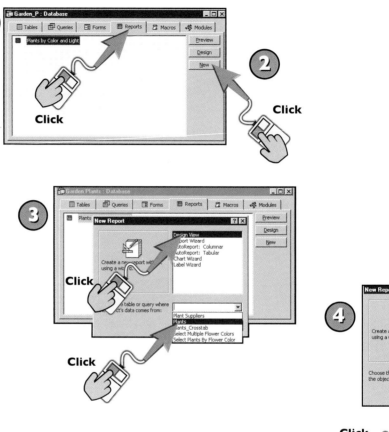

 Maximize the screen
When the Report Design view window is displayed, you should maximize the screen to give yourself the most room possible to work in.

① Click the **Reports** tab on the Database window.

② Click the **New** button.

③ Select **Design View** from the list box. Click on the **Plants** table from the combo box.

④ Click **OK** when you're finished.

Task 3: Adding Fields to the Report

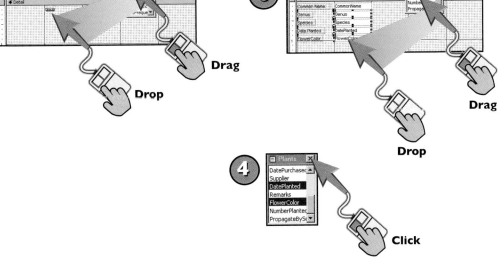

You must add fields to a report so that some sort of information is displayed in the report. As with forms, fields placed on a report display the data from the table or query on which the report is based. Also like a form, fields are placed with both a field and label, both of which can be moved independently of the other.

Click

Drag

Drop

Drag

Drop

Click

① Click the Field List button on the toolbar to open the Field List box.

② Select the field **CommonName** from the list and drag it from the box to the **Detail** grid. The **Detail** grid is the large area below the bar labeled **Detail**.

③ Drag and drop the fields **Genus**, **Species**, **DatePlanted**, and **FlowerColor** onto the **Detail** grid below the **CommonName** field.

④ Close the Field list by clicking its Close (X) button.

✓ **Closing the Field List box**
When the Field List box is displayed in the Design view window, you can close it by clicking the Field List button on the toolbar.

End Task

Task 4: Using Titles

You use titles even more extensively in reports than in forms. Report titles are usually of two types: report titles that are printed once per report and page titles that are printed on each page.

Titles are usually placed in either the **Report Header** or the **Page Header** grid, depending on whether you want them to be displayed once or on every page. A new report always includes a page header but not a report header.

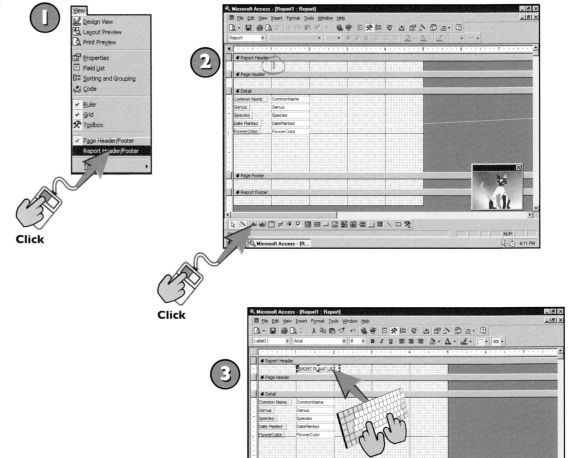

Click

Click

1 Select **View**, **Report Header/Footer** from the menu. Two new grid sections are added to the Design view window, a report header and a report footer.

2 Click the Label button on the toolbox, move the mouse pointer up to the **Report Header** grid, and click once. A very small text box is placed where you clicked.

3 Type **SHORT PLANT LIST** and press Enter to select the label box. Access automatically increases the size of the box as you type.

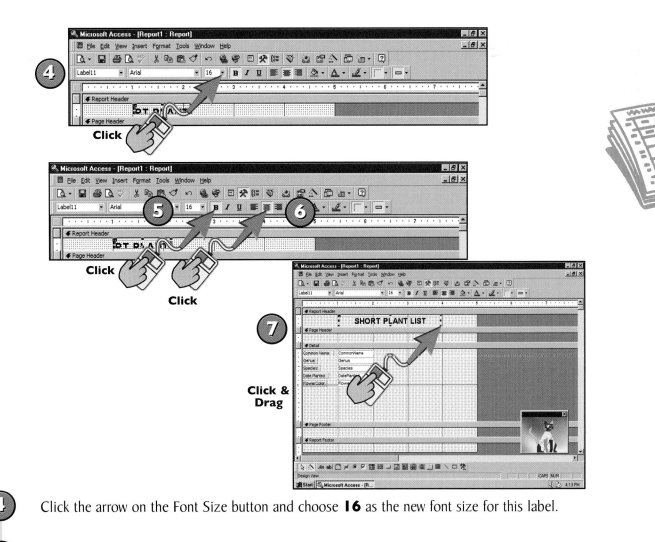

Click

Click

Click

Click &
Drag

SHORT PLANT LIST

4 Click the arrow on the Font Size button and choose **16** as the new font size for this label.

5 Click the Bold button.

6 Click the Center button.

7 Increase the size of the label box by dragging the lower-right handle toward the bottom of the **Page Header** grid and then to the 4-inch line.

End
Task

Task 5: Automatic Page Numbers and Dates

Access can automatically add page numbers and the date and time. You can choose where these will be placed—in the header or footer—and some of the formatting for the item. You can also edit the format of any of them.

Click

Click

Click

Click

Click

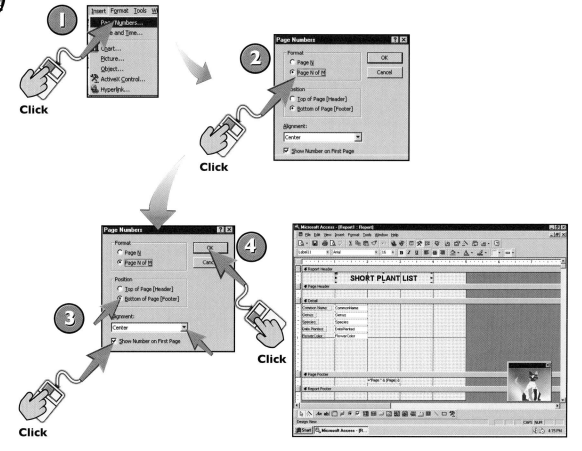

1. Select **Insert**, **Page Numbers**. The Page Numbers dialog box displays.

2. Click the **Page N of M** option button.

3. Click the **Bottom of Page** option button. Select **Center** for the **Alignment**, and be sure that the **Show Number on First Page** check box is checked.

4. Click **OK**. The new text box is placed in the **Page Footer** grid. This will print on every page of the report.

Next Step

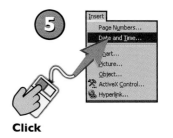

Click

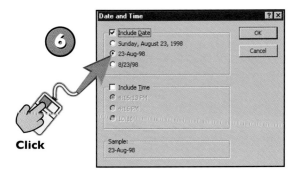

Click

5 Select **Insert**, **Date and Time** from the menu to open the Date and Time dialog box.

6 Click the second option button in the **Include Date** group.

Automatic Page Numbers and Dates Continued

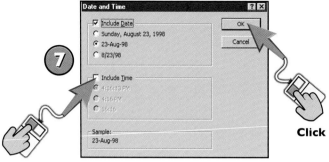

Click

Click

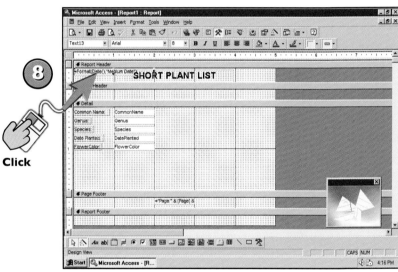

Click

Date and time samples

The sample date and times that you see on your own screen will be different than you see here. They are automatically generated and display the current date and time from your own computer.

7 Uncheck the **Include Time** check box, and click **OK**.

8 The new date text box has been placed in the upper-left corner of the **Report Header** grid. Click it to select it.

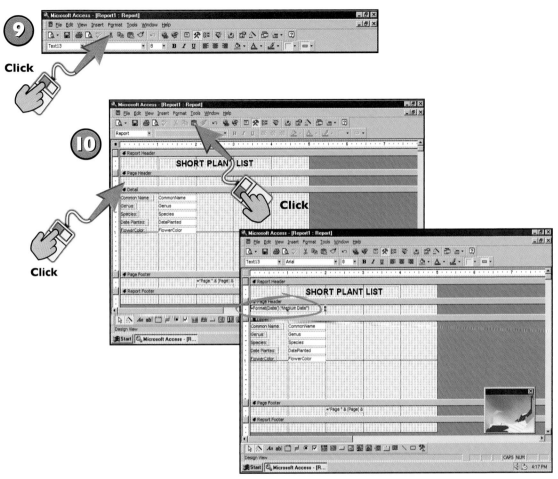

⑨ Click the Cut button on the toolbar. This will remove the new date text box from the **Report Header** grid.

⑩ Click anywhere inside the **Page Header** grid, and then click the Paste button on the toolbar.

✓ **Cut and paste shortcut**
You can also cut a selected object by pressing **Ctrl+X**, and then paste it by pressing **Ctrl+V**.

Task 6: Grouping Records

You can group records in a report instead of printing them in the order they appear in the table or query. Grouping records is a simple way to organize your information. For example, if you were creating a sales report, you might want to group information by region, and then subdivide regions by salesperson. This is a two-level grouping.

Groups not only organize your report; you can also create summary calculations for groups as you can for an entire report.

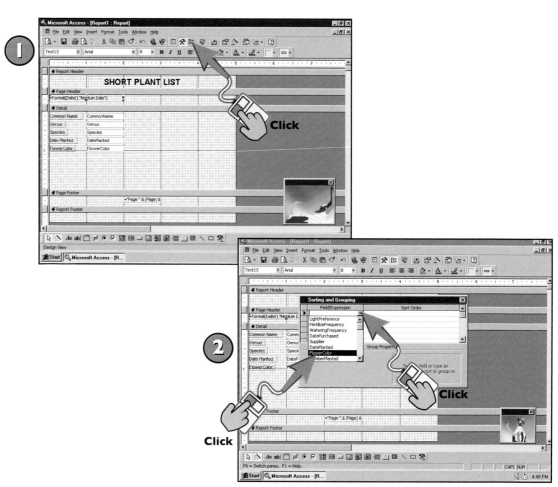

The Yes property
You use the **Group** grid to add information about the group. Leaving these properties set to **No** enables you to sort records by the selected field.

1 Click the Sorting and Grouping button on the toolbar to open the Sorting and Grouping dialog box.

2 Click in the first column and row of the dialog box and click the down arrow button now displayed. Choose the **FlowerColor** field from the drop-down list.

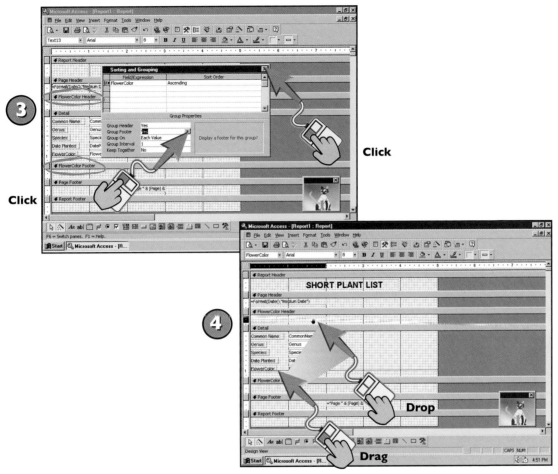

Click

Click

Drop

Drag

3 In the **Group Properties** section select **Yes** for both the **Group Header** and **Group Footer** combo boxes. This creates a **Group** grid on your report. Click the close (X) button.

4 Select and drag the field object **FlowerColor** from the **Detail** grid to the **FlowerColor Header** grid. Be sure to drag the field object and not the label. If you had not yet placed this field in the **Detail** grid, you could also select it from the Field List box and place it in the **Group** grid.

End
Task

Task 7: Sorting Records

In addition to grouping records you can sort records. A report with its information sorted into a recognizable format is much easier to read than one in which the information is simply placed haphazardly into the report.

Groups are always sorted, and you can sort by additional fields within the group.

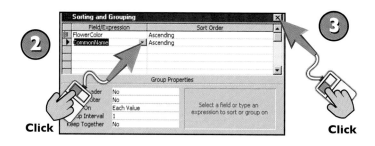

 Click the Sorting and Grouping button to display its dialog box.

 In the second row, click the arrow button and select **CommonName**. Leave the other settings on their default options. This will sort records within each FlowerColor group by the common name of each plant in ascending order.

Close the Sorting and Grouping dialog box by clicking its close (X) button.

Click

Click

4   To see how your report currently looks, click the View button.

5   Click the View button again to return to the Design view window.

Task 8: Moving Field Labels on the Report

When you create a report in Access, field labels are included for each field you place on the report. For most reports, this means that you have a label for each field in the detail section. This can become quite crowded and repetitive on paper.

One way to eliminate this is to move the detail record field labels from beside each field to a group or page header. In this task, you will move the detail record field labels to the FlowerColor group.

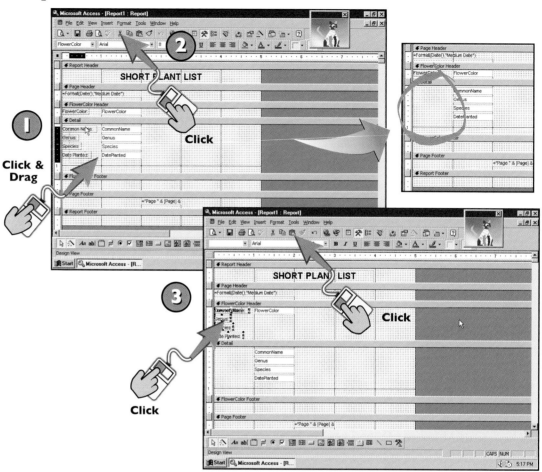

Click &
Drag

Click

1. Select all the detail record field labels by dragging a selection box around them. Be sure not to include any of the fields.

2. Click the Cut button on the toolbar.

3. Click anywhere on the **FlowerColor Header** grid and click the Paste button.

Next Step

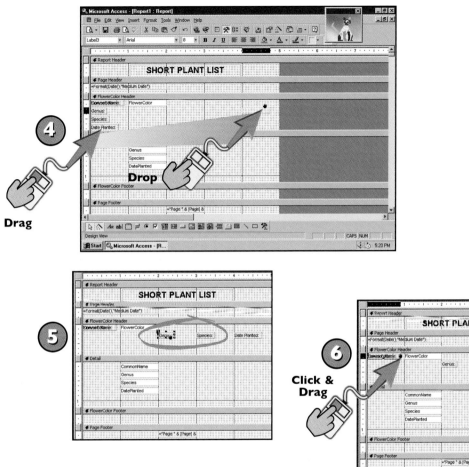

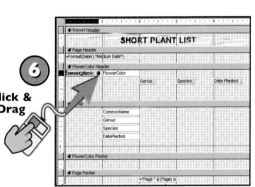

4 Click anywhere in the **FlowerColor Header** area to deselect the four labels, and then click on and drag the **Date Planted** label.

5 Drag the other two visible labels so that they are all to the left of the **Date Planted** label.

6 The **Common Name** label might be hard to get to. It's on top of the **Flower Color** label but is a little longer. The simplest way to move it is to click its right edge and then drag it down.

✓ **Moving labels**
Be careful as you move labels. You don't want someone to misread your report because a label is not aligned with its field.

Task 9: Moving Fields on the Report

After you have moved the field labels so that they are in a horizontal rather than a vertical group, you will want to shift the fields so that they are inline with their own labels.

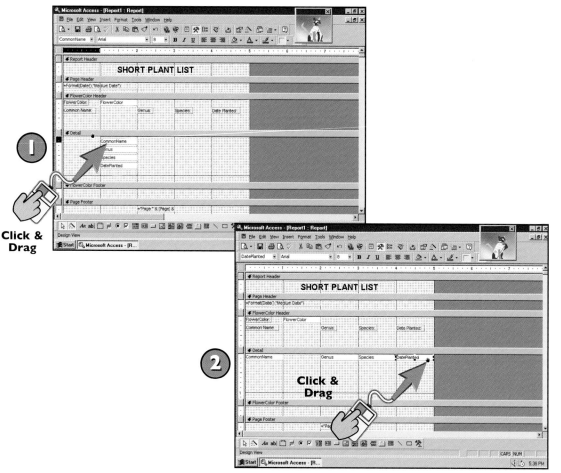

Start Here

Click & Drag

(1) Click the **CommonName** field object and drag it to the left side and to the top of the **Detail** grid.

(2) Select and drag each remaining field so it is directly beneath its label in the **FlowerColor Header** grid, but keep it in the **Detail** grid area.

Next Step

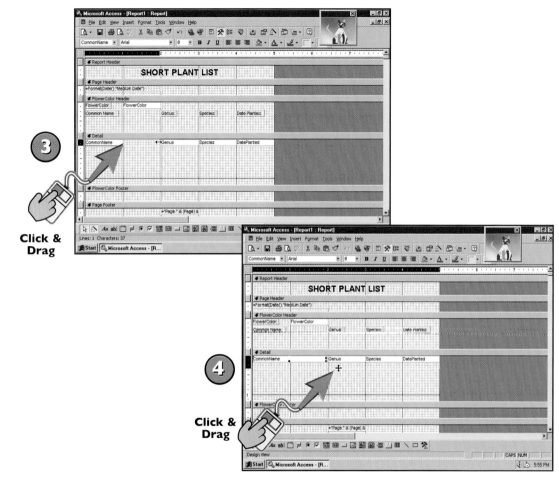

Click & Drag

Click & Drag

③ Some common names are long, so click on and drag the right edge of the **CommonName** field so that it is next to the **Genus** field.

④ Move the mouse pointer to the top edge of the **FlowerColor Footer** bar. Drag the bar up until it touches the detail fields, decreasing the size of the **Detail** grid.

✓ **Note the pointer shape**
The pointer will change shape to a pair of up and down arrows and a horizontal bar when approaching the egde in Step 4.

End Task

Task 10: Calculated Fields in a Report

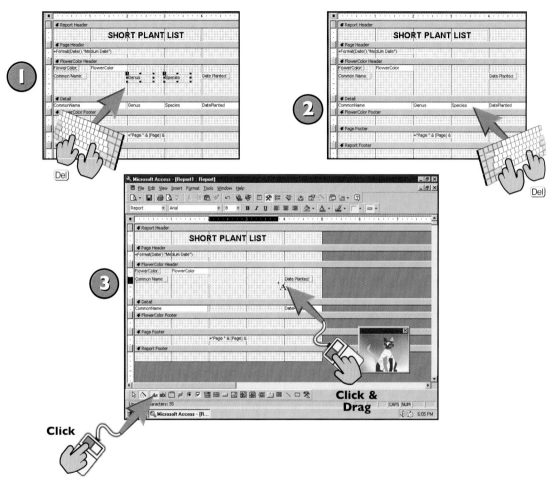

You can use calculated fields in reports for many of the same reasons that you use them in forms. You can calculate values that are not included in a table, or combine information from multiple fields so that a report is easier to read. Calculated fields can also be used for summary information for groups, pages, or the entire report.

In this task, you will delete the **Genus** and **Species** fields and labels and replace them with a calculated text field.

1. Select both the **Genus** and **Species** labels on the **FlowerColor Header** grid and press the Delete key.

2. Select and delete both the **Genus** and **Species** field objects on the **Detail** grid.

3. Click the Label button on the toolbox and drag a new label at the same place on the **FlowerColor Header** grid.

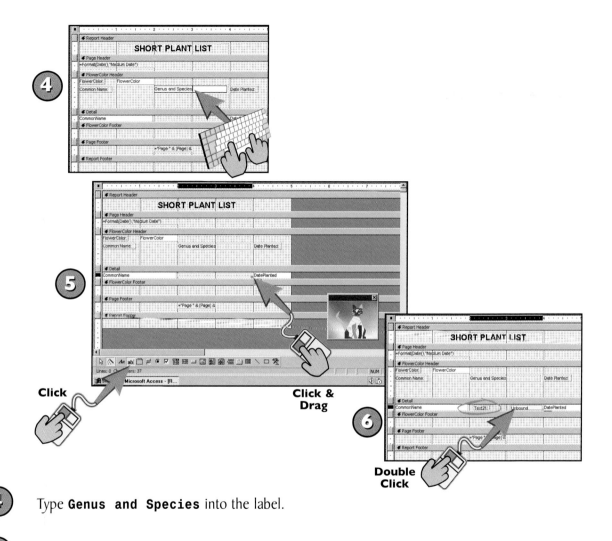

Click

**Click &
Drag**

**Double
Click**

(4) Type **Genus and Species** into the label.

(5) Click the Text Box button on the toolbar and drag a text box where the **Genus** and **Species** field objects had been on the **Detail** grid.

(6) Select and delete the new text box's label. Double-click the new **Unbound** text box, displaying its Property sheet.

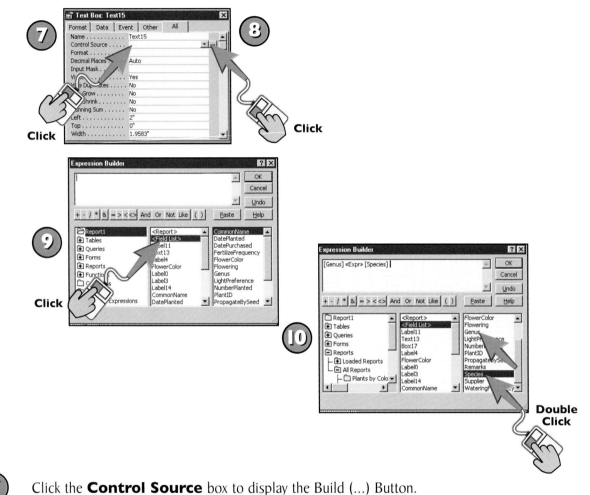

Click the **Control Source** box to display the Build (...) Button.

Click the Build (...) button to display the Expression Builder dialog box.

In the middle list box click the **<Field List>** option. This will display in the right list box a list of all the available fields.

Double-click both the **Genus** and **Species** fields in the list.

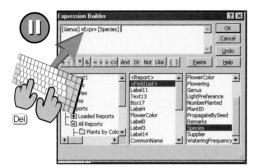

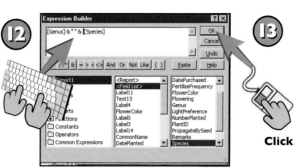

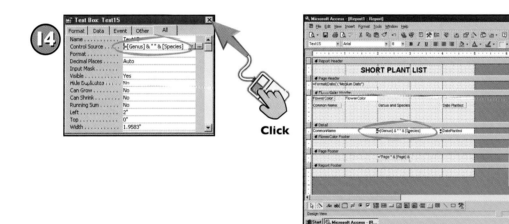

 Select and delete the **Expr** between the two fields in the Expression Builder text box.

 Between the two fields type **&** " " **&** to link these two as a calculated text field.

 Click **OK** on the Expression Builder dialog box. The new formula is entered into the Control Source combo box.

 Close the Property sheet.

Task 11: Adding Special Effects to a Report

There are several special effects that you can apply to both a report's labels and fields. You can draw lines or boxes; use color, shade, or shadows; and change the color of a font. Although there are many things that you can do with a report, don't go totally wild. With a report, always remember the type of printer you will be using. If you are using a laser printer, color will not show up except as patterns and shades of gray. Some colored objects might appear muddied and hard to read. Also, too much color, even when printed on a color printer, can cause a report to print very slowly.

 Select both the **FlowerColor** field object and label.

 Increase the font size from **8** to **12**, and then click the **Bold** button. Increase the size of both objects so that all the text is displayed.

Select the three detail record field labels in the **FlowerColor Header**.

Click the down arrow button beside the **Fill/Back Color** button to display its pallet box. Select the black color box in the upper-left corner.

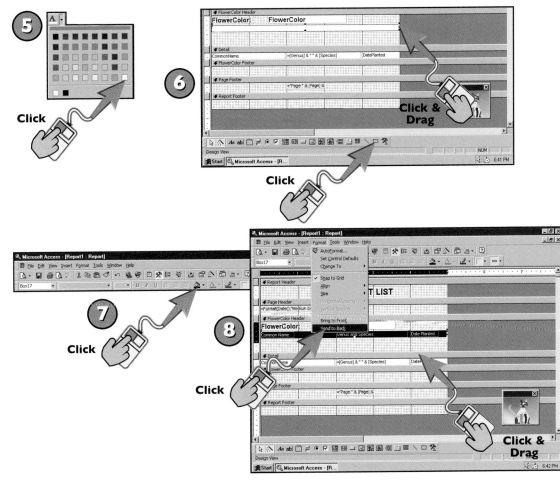

5 Click the down arrow button beside the **Font/Fore Color** button to display its pallet box. Click the white color box in the lower-right corner.

6 Click the Box tool on the toolbox and drag a box around the three labels. When you release the mouse button you will see a box over the labels.

7 Click the **Fill/Back Color** button. This will change the box color to black, which was the last color selected.

8 You still can't see the labels. Click **Format**, **Send to Back** from the menu, and then drag the **Detail** bar up against the bottom of the labels.

Task 12: Viewing a Report

Before you complete a report, especially when you design a new report, you should view it. Look for formatting problems such as whether the report text is all bunched on one side of the page, whether labels and fields are aligned properly, whether there is too much space between elements of the report, and whether the font size and type are appropriate.

If you have used summary calculations in a footer, be sure they are properly labeled and aligned beneath the fields they are summarizing. Sometimes you might need to make number fields smaller in a report in order to align them where you want them.

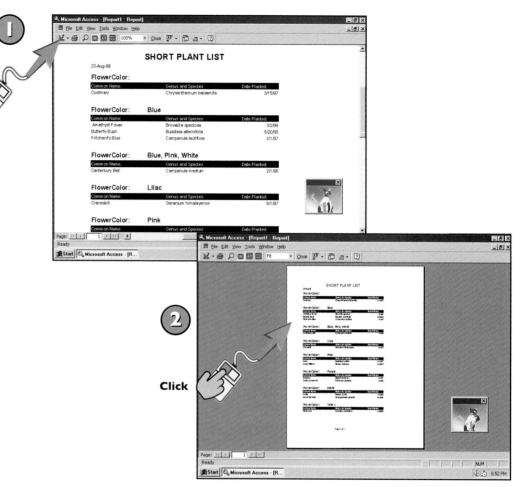

Click

Click

Click the View button on the toolbar. In this view, look at field labels and detail records. Are they well aligned? The label **Date Planted** could be moved to the right.

When looking at a 100% view you might not see page formatting problems. Click the mouse to shrink the page. In this view you can see that the report text is not centered on the page.

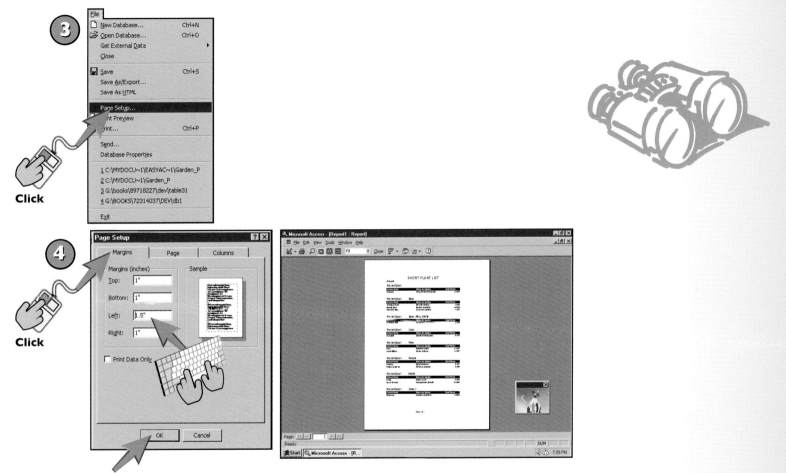

 Click **File**, **Page Setup** to display the Page Setup dialog box.

Click the **Margins** tab and change the **Left** margin from 1 inch to **1.5"** (inches). Click **OK**. The report text has shifted to the right.

Task 13: Saving a Report

After you have created a report that you want to use, you must save it just like any other Access object you create. You then can use it over and over simply by clicking it in the **Reports** tab on the Database window.

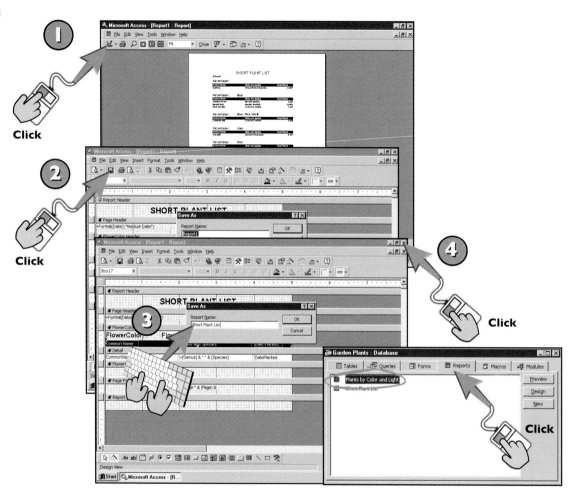

Click

Click

Click

Click

1. Click the View button to return to the Design view window.

2. Click the Save button on the toolbar. The Save As dialog box appears.

3. Type **Short Plant List** and then click **OK**.

4. Click the close (X) button on the Design view window, and then the **Report tab** button on the Database window. You will see your new report listed on the **Reports** tab.

Task 14: Printing a Report

Start Here

In order to easily share a report with others, you must print it. You can view a report onscreen, as you have already done in the Report Preview mode, but this is not the easiest way for several people to see the report.

1

Click

2

Click

3

```
File
  New Database...        Ctrl+N
  Open Database...       Ctrl+O
  Get External Data           ▶
  Close

  Save                   Ctrl+S
  Save As/Export...
  Save As HTML

  Page Setup...
  Print Preview
  Print...               Ctrl+P
  Send...
  Database Properties

  1 C:\MYDOCU~1\EASYAC~1\Garden_P
  2 C:\MYDOCU~1\Garden_P
  3 G:\books\89718227\dev\table31
  4 G:\BOOKS\72314037\DEV\db1

  Exit
```

Click

4

Click

Click

1 Select the **Short Plant List** report in the **Reports** tab list.

2 Click the Print button on the toolbar. When you print this way you don't have the option to specify the number of copies to be printed or to use a printer other than the default printer.

3 To make additional choices when printing a report, select **File**, **Print** from the menu to display the Print dialog box.

4 Make any necessary changes, and click **OK** to print.

End Task

Tables

In Part 3, Task 1, "Entering New Information in a Table," you will need to enter the information contained in the following tables. The tables contain the information needed for the records that you will use throughout the rest of this book. Be sure to enter the information exactly as shown, including mistakes and typos.

Common Name	Genus	Species	Flowering	Light Preference	Fertilize Frequency	Watering Frequency
Amethyst Flower	Browallia	speciosa	Yes ✓	Shade, Filtered Sun	Weekly	Weekly
Butterfly Bbush	buddleia	alternif-olia	Yes ✓	Full Sun	Annually	Keep Dry
Canterbury Bell	Campanula	medium	Yes ✓	Full Sun, Filtered Sun	Monthly	Weekly
Costmary	Chrysanthemum	balsamita	Yes ✓	Full Sun	Monthly	Weekly
Foxglove	Digitalis	purpurea	Yes ✓	Shade, Filtered Sun	Annually	Weekly
Purple Coneflower	Echinacea	purpurea	Yes ✓	Full Sun	Monthly	Weekly
Cranesbill	Geranium	himalayense	Yes ✓	Full Sun	Monthly	Weekly
Lotus	Nelumbo	nucifera	Yes ✓	Full Sun, Filtered Sun	Annually	Keep Wet
catnip	Nepeta	cataria	Yes ✓	Full Sun	Monthly	Weekly
Wormwood	Artemisia	absinthium	Yes ✓	Full Sun	Monthly	Keep Dry

Common Name	Date Propagate	Place Purchased	Date Planted	Remarks	Flower Color	Number Planted	Propagate by Seed
Amethyst Flower	3/1/98	Portland Plants	3/2/98	Annual, may be perennial	Blue	6	Yes ✓
Butterfly Bbush	5/15/95	Portland Plants	5/20/95	Perennial	Blue	2	Yes ✓
Canterbury Bell	12/10/96	Nichol's Plants & Seeds	2/1/96	Biennial	Blue, Pink, White	15	Yes ✓
Costmary	3/15/97	NW Hardy Plants	3/15/97	Perennial	3	No	
Foxglove	5/1/94	N/A	6/1/94	Biennial, perennial	Purple	12	Yes ✓
Purple Coneflower	3/1/96	Portland Plants	3/2/96	Perennial	Purple	3	Yes ✓
Cranesbill	6/1/97	St. John's Perennials	6/1/97	Perennial	Lilac	2	Yes ✓
Lotus	3/15/97	Portland Pond's	3/15/97	Perennial	Pink	2	No
catnip	6/1/95	St. John's Perennials	6/3/95	Perennial	White	6	Yes ✓
Wormwood	4/15/96	St. John's Perennials	4/20/96	Perennial	Yellow	1	Yes ✓

The following table contains the information you need for Part 3, Task 2, "Completing the Supplier Table."

Supplier	Address	City	State	Zip/Postal Code	Telephone	Catalog Only
St. John's Perennials	111 N. Main	Portland	OR	97222	(503) 555-4231	(empty)
Portland Plants	42567 NW 23rd	Portland	OR	97333	(503) 555-8763	(empty)
NW Hardy Plants	PO Box 309548	Vancouver	WA	98456	(360) 555-9834	Check
Nichol's Plants & Seeds	Star Rt 4 NW	McMinnville	OR	96589	(541) 555-9988	(empty)

Symbols

INFO

T